Costa Blanca

COLLINS
Glasgow & London

First published 1990
Copyright © William Collins Sons & Company Limited
Printed and Published by
William Collins Sons & Company Limited
ISBN 0 00 435772-8

HOW TO USE THIS BOOK

Your Collins Traveller Guide will help you find your way around your chosen destination quickly and easily. It is colour-coded for easy reference:

The blue-coded 'topic' section answers the question 'I would like to see or do something; where do I go and what do I see when I get there?'
A simple, clear layout provides an alphabetical list of activities and events, offers you a selection of each, tells you how to get there, what it will cost, when it is open and what to expect. Each topic in the list has its own simplified map, showing the position of each item and the nearest landmark or transport access, for instant orientation. Whether your interest is Architecture or Food you can find all the information you need quickly and simply. Where major resorts within an area require in-depth treatment, they follow the main topics section in alphabetical order.

The red-coded section is a lively and informative gazetteer. In one alphabetical list you can find essential facts about the main places and cultural items - 'What is La Bastille?', 'Who was Michelangelo?' - as well as practical and invaluable travel information. It covers everything you need to know to help you enjoy yourself and get the most out of your time away, from Accommodation through Babysitters, Car Hire, Food, Health, Money, Newspapers, Taxis and Telephones to Zoos.

Cross-references: Type in small capitals - CHURCHES - tells you that more information on an item is available within the topic on churches. A-Z in bold - **A-Z** - tells you that more information is available on an item within the gazetteer. Simply look under the appropriate heading. A name in bold - **Holy Cathedral** - also tells you that more information on an item is available in the gazetteer under that particular heading.

Packed full of information and easy to use - you'll always know where you are with your Collins Traveller Guide!

Photographs by **Keith Allardyce**
Cover picture by **Travel Photo International**

INTRODUCTION

If pressed to specify just two ingredients essential to flavour a holiday, most Britons would opt for fun and sun. And that, in a nutshell, is why the Costa Blanca is the destination of so many charter aircraft leaving the UK. This area of mainland Spain knows exactly how to cater for our tastes.

The rugged coastline is well-endowed with three natural resources: sea, sand and sunshine. For centuries, the folk of the coastal villages eked a living from fishing. Some still do so, and a holiday at one of the picturesque hamlets is ideal for those who simply want to relax, recharge the batteries, and watch the world go by. But it is a fortnight in the fast lane that attracts most folk to this Costa.

Tourism, the biggest growth industry of the past few decades, has brought power to the peseta and the people. The economic resurrection transformed their way of life and the landscape. The business has mushroomed beyond the wildest dreams of even the most optimistic Spanish entrepreneur and, as a result, the land has grown accommodation of every size and shape to suit every desire and budget. Fly Club Class to one of the expensive five-star hotels and have your every whim tended to hand and foot, or 'do it on the cheap', travelling overland on a bus and fixing up a self-catering apartment on arrival.

The Costa Blanca, or White Coast, is so called because of the white, sandy beaches which sparkle in the brilliant light along 270 km of the Mediterranean. It is a sun-worshippers' paradise, with an average of nine hours sunshine a day and 70°F in April rising to 12 hours a day and a sizzling 88°F in July and August. Those entrusted with the task of building up the new industry and attracting holiday-makers recognized the lure of the sun and set out to lay firm foundations for the fun.

Benidorm, the principal resort of the Costa Blanca, is the Blackpool of the Mediterranean. It throbs with events and excitement practically 24 hours a day, with sport, recreation and amusement for young and old, energetic and easy-going. If you want a quiet holiday, look elsewhere. This resort has no pretensions - it is for those who want to enjoy themselves and have no objections to others doing the same. It is swimming, sunbathing, and shopping during the day, and music, discos and dancing at night. 'Night' is a vague term, beginning at sundown and continuing until it rises. I should say that one major recreation is drinking - at

any hour of the day or night. If you have a thirst, the bars and cafés are there to quench it. Prices vary, but follow the strains of *Una Paloma Blanca* for a good deal. As the pesetas diminish, which they tend to do with alarming haste, bottles of spirits may beckon from supermarkets, at around £3 a litre. There are plenty of chemist's shops to provide the antidote.

Britons flocked to this Costa early in its new 'career', so it evolved catering to their tastes. If one of the items high on your list of necessities is good food, you will find plenty to please your palate. Hotels and cafés have 'British menus', beginning with full English breakfast and going through the card to roast beef, spuds and two veg. Almost everyone speaks English, although in translation traders' arithmetic has been known to be inaccurate. Wrong, as they say, in the right way. Shop around because prices do vary. And check your change - often an error cannot be rectified later. In English or Spanish, a rogue's a rogue, and who's going to let him spoil the holiday? But, rest assured, this is the exception rather than the rule. The vast majority of locals work in the tourist industry and they are not likely to bite the hand that feeds them.

Package holiday companies and local businessmen offer a wide variety of day trips and evening excursions at reasonable prices. Choose

between a sedate cruise on the Med or a swashbuckling sail in a pirate ship, ending invariably with a precarious walk along the plank. Visit a lace factory or a vineyard. The medieval evenings are great fun, with ye olde knights fighting it out 'to the death'. The horseback jousting is spectacular. Listen to sword clang against sword, feel the swish of the mace as you tuck into suckling pig and drink mead. At around £15, including transport, these events offer exceptional value.

The mild Mediterranean weather allows the Costa Blanca to remain open for business all year round. It offers extended winter holidays at reduced rates, aimed specifically at pensioners who find that the savings to be made, particularly in heavy heating bills, go a long way towards meeting the cost of leaving Britain's icy shores for a much warmer, and healthier climate. The locals lay on entertainment tailored to their needs, but come spring, as the temperature rises so does the tempo and the influx of package holiday-makers begins afresh. For some it will be the best holiday abroad, as it is for many who return year after year.

William Coffey

PLAYA DE VERGEL 8 km west of Denia.
*Large, quiet, sandy bay incorporating Deveses, Palmars and Almadraba beaches. Restaurants and windsurfing school at La Felicidad - enquire at Urbanización La Felicidad. Blue flag (see **Beaches**).*

LAS MARINAS 2 km west of Denia.
*A long, wide stretch of fine sand with good water sports facilities. Restaurants and bars across the road. Blue flag (see **Beaches**).*

LES ROTES (LAS ROTAS) / PLAYA DE DENIA
4 km east of Denia.
*Sandy beaches at the town end, served by water sports and restaurants. Rocky coves towards Cabo de San Antonio. Blue flag (see **Beaches**).*

PLAYA GRAVA / PLAYA BENISERO
2 km east of Jávea town centre.
*Long, grey sandy beach on main road next to Jávea (see **RESORT REVIEW 1**, **A-Z**). Built-up backdrop of hotels and restaurants. Scuba-diving at the port.*

PLAYA DEL ARENAL (PLAYA DE LA ARENA)
5 km south east of Jávea town centre.
Pleasant, sandy, 1-km-long family beach. Busy promenade lined with restaurants and bars. Water sports available.

PLAYA PORTICHOL / PLAYA LA BARRACA
10 km south east of Jávea town centre.
Small and secluded sandy coves accessible from the narrow, winding road to Cabo de la Nao. Excellent for scuba-diving.

PLAYA DE AMBOLO
West of Cabo de la Nao (signposted Urbanización La Siesta).
Small coves designated as naturist beaches, although you don't have to bare all to enjoy this secluded spot.

PLAYA DE GRANADELLA 2 km west of Cabo de la Nao.
Small, scenic, pebble beach with restaurants, framed by lovely pine woods.

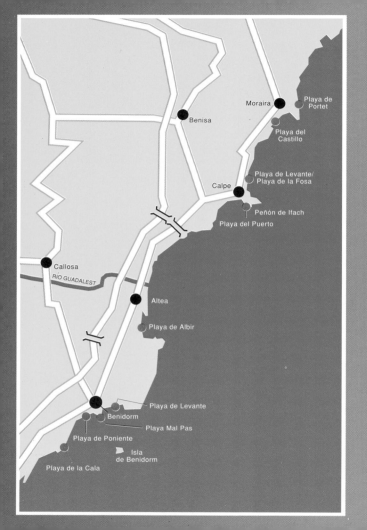

Moraira-Benidorm

PLAYA DE PORTET 1 km east of Moraira.
Attractive, quiet, sand and pebble beach backed by hills and villas.
Restaurants and windsurfing.

PLAYA DEL CASTILLO 1 km south of Moraira yachting harbour.
Windsurfing and sailing are available from this safe, sheltered, family beach,
lined with restaurants.

PLAYA DE LEVANTE / PLAYA DE LA FOSA
Immediately north of Peñón de Ifach.
2 km of wide, sandy beach serving the resort of Calpe (see RESORT REVIEW 1,
A-Z). Bars, restaurants, children's amusements and water sports.

PLAYA DEL PUERTO Immediately south of Peñón de Ifach.
Attractive fishing harbour with two small sandy beaches, bars, restaurants
and shops. Sports facilities are limited.

PLAYA DE ALBIR 2 km south of Altea.
The best of several long pebbly beaches serving Altea (see RESORT REVIEW 1,
A-Z), lined with camping sites and hotels.

PLAYA DE LEVANTE East of Benidorm town centre.
One of Europe's most popular beaches, this magnificent 2-km stretch of
sand is cleaned daily and offers every tourist facility.

PLAYA MAL PAS Benidorm old town - foot of Balcón de Mer.
Small sandy beach with no facilities but ideal for a relaxing doze in the sun
if it's not too busy.

PLAYA DE PONIENTE West of Benidorm town centre.
A similarly high standard to Levante, the 3 km of sand here is quieter and
particularly attractive at its southern tip.

PLAYA DE LA CALA Montbenidorm, 3 km south of Benidorm.
Most peaceful of the main beaches near Benidorm (see RESORT REVIEW 1, A-
Z), this sandy cove is well served by restaurants and water sports facilities.

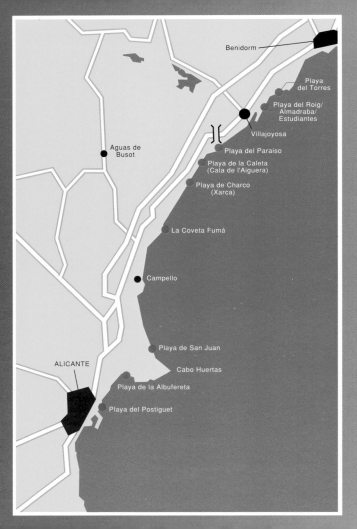

Villajoyosa-Alicante

PLAYA DEL TORRES 4 km east of Villajoyosa.
Popular beach with local camping grounds, a mix of sand and rocks lined by trees. Windsurfing available, good area for scuba-diving.

PLAYA DEL ROIG / ALMADRABA / ESTUDIANTES
1 km east from port of Villajoyosa, signposted Estudiantes.
Small, quiet bays with shingle, fine sand and pebble beaches. Some bars.

PLAYA DEL PARAISO 4 km west of Villajoyosa.
Narrow, fine-sand beach over 1 km long and well serviced with bars and restaurants.

PLAYA DE LA CALETA (CALA DE L'AIGUERA)
6 km west of Villajoyosa, signposted next to Montiboli Hotel.
Small, quiet beach of tiny pebbles, dotted with palm trees. Tennis courts at the hotel plus windsurfing, sailing and scuba-diving equipment for hire.

PLAYA DE CHARCO (XARCA)
8 km west of Villajoyosa, 1 km off main road by El Charco restaurant.
Small, quiet, rocky cove with sandy beach and clear, shallow water.

LA COVETA FUMÁ
2 km north of Campello, 1 km off main road signposted to 'Ian's Place'.
Small, secluded, rocky bay set amidst pretty villas.

PLAYA DE SAN JUAN 7 km north of Alicante.
Very long beach with fine sand to the south, rocks and shingle to the north. Well developed and lined with restaurants, bars and hotels.

PLAYA DE LA ALBUFERETA 3 km north of Alicante.
Small, fine-sand beach with palm trees, overlooked by high-rise apartments and restaurants. Water sports available.

PLAYA DEL POSTIGUET Alicante centre.
Soft-sand beach with palm trees, often crowded by the locals. Fashionable promenade lined with bars and restaurants. Water sports available.

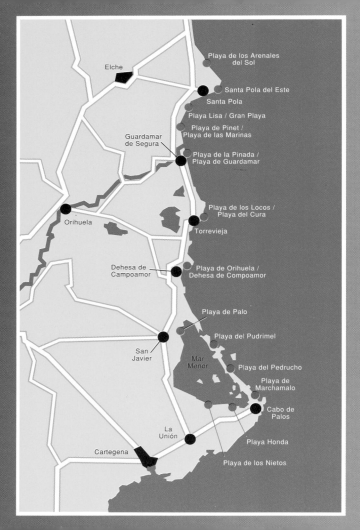

Playa de los Arenales del Sol

Santa Pola del Este

Santa Pola

Playa Lisa / Gran Playa

Playa de Pinet / Playa de las Marinas

Elche

Guardamar de Segura

Playa de la Pinada / Playa de Guardamar

Playa de los Locos / Playa del Cura

Orihuela

Torrevieja

Dehesa de Campoamor

Playa de Orihuela / Dehesa de Compoamor

Playa de Palo

Playa del Pudrimel

San Javier

Mar Menor

Playa del Pedrucho

Playa de Marchamalo

Cabo de Palos

La Unión

Playa Honda

Cartegena

Playa de los Nietos

PLAYA DE LOS ARENALES DEL SOL 9 km north of Santa Pola.
Long beaches of fine golden sand backed by dunes and urbanización (see
A-Z). *Restaurants and sports facilities.*

SANTA POLA DEL ESTE 2 km north of Santa Pola.
Small rocky bays back onto the quiet, pretty urbanización (see **A-Z**) *of
Santa Pola del Este. Sports facilities at El Torreón centre.*

PLAYA LISA / GRAN PLAYA Immediately west of Santa Pola.
*Long, grey sandy beaches with limited tourist facilities, but some water
sports. They can get crowded with locals.*

PLAYA DE PINET / PLAYA DE LAS MARINAS
10 km south of Santa Pola.
Long, fine-sand beach backed by pine forest. Few facilities at southern end.

PLAYA DE LA PINADA / PLAYA DE GUARDAMAR
Guardamar del Segura.
Gently duned beach. Most facilities to the north. Blue flag (see **Beaches**).

PLAYA DE LOS LOCOS / PLAYA DEL CURA
Immediately east of Torrevieja port.
Small sandy bays divided by Punta Carral. Backed by hotels and restaurants.

PLAYAS DE ORIHUELA / DEHESA DE CAMPOAMOR
10 km south of Torrevieja.
*White sandy beach stretching for half a km with water sports facilities in
the middle of an urbanización (see* **A-Z**).

PLAYA DE PALO / LOS NIETOS / PLAYA HONDA
Mar Menor (lagoon side).
Quiet, long, fine sand, very shallow water, excellent water sports facilities.

PLAYA DE MARCHAMALO / PEDRUCHO / PUDRIMEL
La Manga del Mar Menor (Mediterranean side).
Long sandy beaches stretching some 14 km and backed by high-rise hotels.

BASKETRY AND WICKERWORK

As the central town of Europe's largest palm forest, Elche (see **A-Z**) special-
izes in basketry, as does the village of Gata de Gorgos (see **EXCURSION 1**).
Hats, sombreros, baskets and boxes are available.

CARPETS AND BLANKETS

Crevillente is famous for woollen blankets, woven rugs and carpets, which
can be purchased from the factories at very reasonable prices.

CERAMICS

The famous Lladró chinaware and attractive Mudéjar (Moresque) ceramics
from Manises, near Valencia (see **A-Z**), are ubiquitous in local gift shops.

FASHION

Spanish fashions, for men and women, are as good as anywhere in Europe.
The larger towns have a good range of fashion shops, particularly for shoes.

GLASSWARE

Amber, green and purple Crevillente glassware is widely available.

LEATHER GOODS

Elche (see **A-Z**) is the main centre for the shoe industry and fine leather
goods are to be found everywhere - bags, shoes, jackets, coats, belts, etc.

TURRÓN

Turrón is a type of nougat largely made in Jijona which supplies the whole
country with this Arabic delicacy made from almonds and honey. Buy from
El Lobo factory (see **EXCURSION 4**) or El Altet duty-free shop (see **Airport**).

WINES

The Costa Blanca's famous Moscatel is deliciously sweet and the Jalón area
produces good red and rosé wines. See **Drinks**, **A-Z**.

WOOL

Woollens, blankets, sweaters, shawls and ponchos are sold all along the
Costa as well as in tourist villages like Guadalest (see **EXCURSION 2**, **A-Z**).

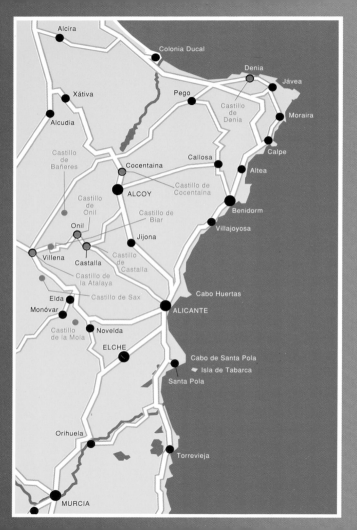

CASTILLO DE BAÑERES 21 km west of Alcoy.
This well-restored 12thC castle dominates one hill above Alcoy (see **EXCURSION 4**, **A-Z***) and La Ermita del Cristo (hermitage) occupies the other.*

CASTILLO DE DENIA 58 km north east of Benidorm.
•0900-1330, 1700-2000 (Museum).
Situated on a hill overlooking Denia (see **RESORT REVIEW 1**, **A-Z***), this castle was originally constructed by the Romans. See* **EXCURSION 1**, **MUSEUMS**.

CASTILLO DE SAX 48 km west of Alicante.
Sited on a clifftop and including a museum of fiesta costumes. Construction was started by the Romans and completed by the Arabs. See **EXCURSION 3**.

CASTILLO DE LA ATALAYA Villena, 63 km west of Alicante.
Originally built by the Arabs in the 12thC and with a similar structure to the Castillo de Biar. See **EXCURSION 3**.

CASTILLO DE LA MOLA near Novelda, 33 km west of Alicante.
This castle, dating from the early Christian period, has a unique triangular tower. See **EXCURSION 3**.

CASTILLO DE BIAR 7 km east of Villena.
This well-conserved Moorish castle has dungeons and a small archeological museum. See **EXCURSION 3**.

CASTILLO DE CASTALLA 18 km east of Villena.
Overlooks the town of Castalla. In the town La Ermita de la Sangre (hermitage) dates from the 14thC and has a Gothic nave supported by a diaphragm of arches. See **EXCURSION 3 & 4**.

CASTILLO DE ONIL 18 km east of Villena.
Acts as the local town hall. One of the four towers is occupied by the parish church which is also the palace of the Marqués de Dos Aguas.

CASTILLO DE COCENTAINA 7 km north of Alcoy.
This fortress has been attacked many times during its history.

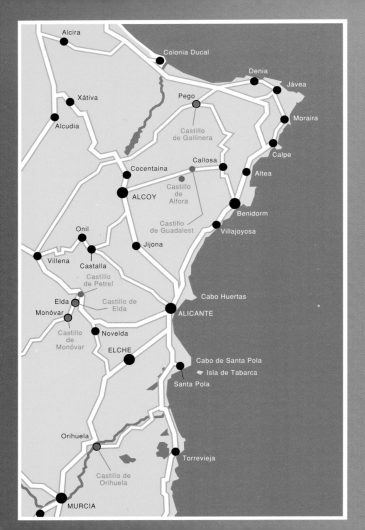

CASTILLO DE ELDA 38 km west of Alicante.
This huge 14thC Gothic castle dominates the centre of Elda and has shel-
tered up to 4000 persons.

CASTILLO DE PETREL 38 km west of Alicante.
This 12thC Moorish castle in the town of Petrel is currently being restored.
See EXCURSION 3.

CASTILLO DE ORIHUELA
55 km south west of Alicante.
The remains of a monumental fortress with over 100 towers in the cathedral
town of Orihuela (see **A-Z***).*

CASTILLO DE MONÓVAR 37 km west of Alicante.
Hexagonal-shaped castle. The tower of Homenaje, near the entrance, was
once dominated by two other towers.

CASTILLO DE GUADALEST 28 km north west of Benidorm.
Inaccessible except for a tunnel through 15 m of solid rock. Guadalest was
never conquered and remains one of the area's main attractions. Two other
castles, Castillo del Rey and Castillo de la Alcorzaiba, overlook the valley
and lake. See EXCURSION 2, MUSTS, **Guadalest**.

CASTILLO DE GALLINERA
near Benirrama, 30 km west of Denia.
This castle was destroyed by an earthquake in 1644. It is difficult to reach
and only certain parts of the walls and a circular tower can be visited.

CASTILLO DE ALFORA
near Confrides, 28 km north west of Benidorm.
Located on a high mountain, this castle has ruined towers which dominate
the Guadalest valley.

Castillo de Guadalest

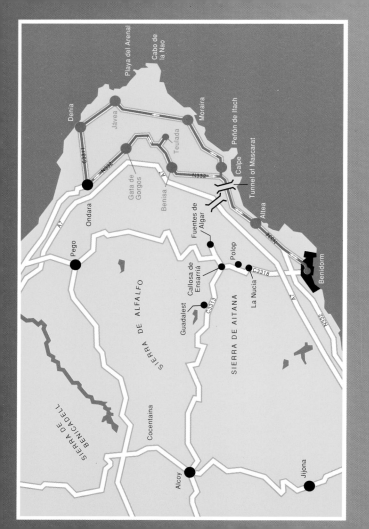

Coastal Towns

83 km. A one-day round trip to some of the northern Costa Blanca's most popular towns. Best time: early Tuesday, to visit Altea market en route.

Starting from Benidorm, head north on the N 332 in the direction of Valencia (see **A-Z**).

10 km - Altea (see **MUSTS**, **RESORT REVIEW 1**, **A-Z**). This is one of the best examples of an unspoilt coastal town on the whole of the Costa Blanca. Turn left off the main road, park the car and walk up the hill heading towards the blue domed Iglesia Virgen del Consuelo. As there are some 250 steps this climb is not for the elderly or infirm but the panoramic views and the charming atmosphere (reminiscent of the Sacré Cœur in Paris) makes the effort worthwhile.

Resume the journey along the N 332 and as it continues to climb you will come across some dramatic and beautiful sea-views. Stop just before the Tunnel of Mascarat (5 km) to admire the particularly deep rich blue of the sea. Continue for a further 3 km before turning off right towards Calpe.

21 km - Calpe (see **RESORT REVIEW 1**, **A-Z**). Before heading downhill on one of Calpe's long main roads towards the Peñón de Ifach explore the narrow whitewashed streets of the old town huddled around the church at the top of the hill. Although it may look daunting, the Peñón de Ifach (see **WALK 4**, **A-Z**), which towers 327 m high, can quite easily be scaled by anyone of average fitness. It is covered in wild flowers and often rewards climbers with sightings of rare birds. The port and small beaches on the south side of the Peñón are worth a visit (see **BEACHES 2**). Continue along the picturesque coast road towards Moraira.

32 km - Moraira. The main attractions here are the two excellent beaches. See **BEACHES 2**.

Continuing along the same road towards Jávea you will cross the Sierra Benitachell, rich with orange and lemon groves.

47 km - Jávea (see **RESORT REVIEW 1**, **A-Z**). Take the signs *centro ciudad*. Jávea's delightful old town is crowded by whitewashed houses with arched porches, Gothic windows and wrought iron balconies. Visit the fortress church, built in 1513, the Museo Histórico y Etnográfico (see **MUSEUMS**) and the excellent Casa de Cultura for a drink and snack with the local people. If it is siesta time (see **A-Z**) and the church and muse-

Iglesia Virgen del Consuelo, Altea

um are closed you may wish to head instead for the beach at Playa del Arenal (see **BEACHES 1**), signposted *Parador Nacional*. From the centre of Jávea old town take the road signposted towards Denia. This dramatic route of steep hairpin bends provides good material for the keen amateur photographer.

56 km - Denia (see **RESORT REVIEW 1, A-Z**). The main attraction in Denia, aside from its beaches (see **BEACHES 1**), is the 18thC castle which rises to a height of 58 m and gives excellent views (see **CASTLES 1**). Inside is the Museo Arqueológico (see **MUSEUMS**), and at the foot of the castle, an 18thC church, the Iglesia de Santa María. From Denia turn left, away from the coast road, onto the C 3311 towards Ondara, then take the N 332 to Gata de Gorgos.

Altea

71 km - Gata de Gorgos. The main through-road of this small town is lined with shops selling basketry (see **BEST BUYS**) and local wares.

7 km outside Gata de Gorgos turn left onto the C 1343. After 1 km you will arrive in Teulada.

79 km - Teulada. Walk around the central streets of this small and attractive old town and see the 17thC Ermita Divina Pastora.

Return to the N 332 and go 5 km to Benisa.

83 km - Benisa. The old part of Benisa is a good example of a well-preserved Moorish town. Its interesting old buildings include a 17thC convent and the Museo Histórico y Etnográfico. Visit the Casa de Cultura for refreshments.

Return to Benidorm on the N 332 or alternatively by joining the A 7 motorway at junction 63.

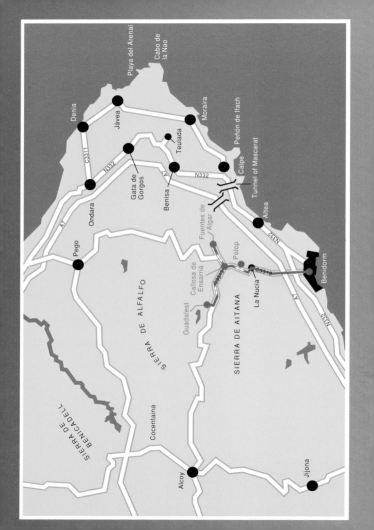

Inland Towns

60 km. *A one-day trip through magnificent scenery and charming villages to see the Costa Blanca's most impressive castle community. Best time: early Tuesday, to visit the market at Callosa de Ensarriá and avoid the coach crowds at Guadalest.*

Starting from Benidorm, take the C 3318 towards Callosa de Ensarriá and pass through La Nucia.

12km - Polop. Sitting in the middle of a huge orchard, Polop's claim to local fame is its large rectangular water fountain spouting 221 taps. Walk up the hill to the top of the ruined castle. This has been converted into a cemetery which is now overgrown and dilapidated. Its catacombs (resembling deep ovens) are empty, as is the ruined medieval jail cave. Rejoin the C 3318.

17 km - Callosa de Ensarriá. This attractive old town holds a lively market on Tuesday mornings in the main square next to the 14thC church (see **Market Days**). The Arrabal art gallery is signposted, just a short walk around the corner. It contains an interesting collection of varying modern pieces (closed during siesta - see **A-Z**).

Leave Callosa on the C 3313 and sweep up through the magnificent mountain scenery. After a few kilometres you will come to a roadside stall outside El Riu bar. Here you can sample the local honey, *Moscatel* and other local wines. See **Drinks**, **Wine**.

28 km - Guadalest (see **CASTLES 2**, **MUSTS**, **A-Z**). Built by the Moors some 1200 years ago this mountain-top castle village now houses a community which thrives on tourism. It can only be entered by an archway carved out of the mountain side and has never been taken by force. The views from here are breathtaking and the village itself is extremely well preserved. Go into the 12thC prison and visit the ruined castle, as at Polop converted into a cemetery, but here still in use. Return to Callosa by the same road and turn left towards Pego. After 2.5 km you will see a sign downhill to the right to Fuentes de Algar.

42 km - Fuentes de Algar. A picturesque 25 m high waterfall which provides a pleasant backdrop for a picnic. You can also have a dip in the bracing waters of the little pool at the foot of the waterfall. In high season there are donkey rides around the area.

Return again to Callosa and take the C 3318 back to Benidorm.

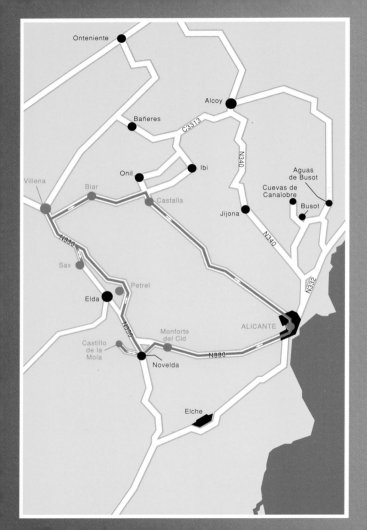

Route of the Castles

121 km. A one-day drive back into history visiting six of Alicante Province's medieval castles. Best time: early morning, to miss the siesta.

Starting from Alicante, take the N 330 towards Madrid.

26 km - Monforte del Cid. Visit the splendid Gothic church which was restyled in the 18thC. After 2 km take a left turn to Novelda and after another 2 km take the second road on the right, signposted to Castillo de la Mola (3 km).

33 km - Castillo de la Mola (see CASTLES 1). The unique triangular tower of these Moorish remains dates from the 13thC. Next to the ruins perched on the edge of the hilltop is the remarkable bright pink 19thC sanctuary of La Magdalena, looking just like a gingerbread castle on the banks of the Rhine! Go back down the hill, take the first left, then left again back onto the N 330 towards Madrid.

48 km - Petrel (see CASTLES 2). The 12thC castle towers over the old part of this medieval town. It is a steep climb up to the foot of the castle (no entry as it is currently under restoration) but the inside keep and walls are still impressive and there are fine views over Petrel from here.

58 km - Sax (see CASTLES 1). The impressive, well-preserved medieval castle (with Roman origins) sits 500 m above the old town. It is best admired from below as it is a very long, steep climb, and inaccessible by car. If you do make it to the top, the castle is open by request 1700-1900 Mon.-Fri., 1200-1400, 1700-1900 Sat., Sun. & hols.

72 km - Villena. The 12thC Castillo de la Atalaya (see CASTLES 1) is said to be one of the finest examples of medieval military architecture in Spain. For admission apply to the Ayuntamiento (Town Hall). See the town's unique Bronze Age Iberian treasures in the Museo Arqueológico inside the 16thC Ayuntamiento, open daily. Return to the N 330 and head for a short way back towards Alicante before turning left to Biar.

73 km - Biar (see CASTLES 1). The attractive Castillo de Biar was built by the Moors c. 1100, and is open to the public. In the old town square is the Iglesia de la Asunción with its splendid Gothic facade. Continue through Biar towards Ibi and after 10 km turn right towards Castalla.

85 km - Castalla (see CASTLES 1, EXCURSION 4). The ruined, inaccessible castle is an impressive landmark. Visit La Ermita de la Sangre, which dates from the 14thC. Follow the road back to Alicante (36 km).

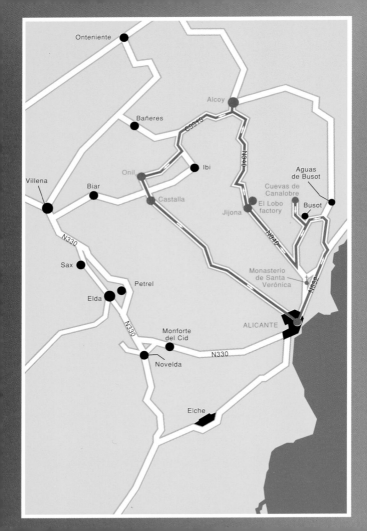

West of Alicante

133 km. *A one-day drive inland to an historic monastery, magnificent caves, a turrón factory and a fine old city. Best time: leave early enough to arrive in Alcoy before the siesta. You may wish to omit Jijona on the way out and see it on the way back instead of seeing Onil and Castalla.*

Starting from Alicante, take the N 332 towards Valencia (see **A-Z**).

5 km - Monasterio de Santa Verónica ('La Santa Faz'). See **ALICANTE 2**. The 15thC monastery takes its popular name, which means 'The Holy Face', from a relic claimed to be part of a cloth used by St Veronica to wipe Christ's brow at Calvary. It is kept in a silver container at the high altar. Rejoin the N 332 and after 3 km turn left towards Aguas de Busot. After 7 km turn left towards Busot, then right after 5 km.

25 km - Cuevas de Canalobre (see **MUSTS**). This remarkable, recently-discovered cave is over 100 million years old and is one of Spain's greatest natural treasures. Go back down the hill for 3 km and take the road to Jijona. After another 10 km turn right to join the N 340.

41 km - Jijona. Visit the splendid 14thC Gothic church in the town centre with its two Baroque chapels. Continue on the N 340 through Jijona and 1 km on the right is the El Lobo *turrón* factory (see **BEST BUYS**). Take a tour of the factory and museum (0930-1330, 1600-1930 every 30 min; donation to charity expected) and buy some *turrón* from their shop. Continue north through a series of mountains and ravines.

69 km - Alcoy (see **A-Z**). The town is spectacularly divided by ravines. Drive to the old part (signposted *centro ciudad*) and park off the Plaza de España. Walk down the Pintor Casanova to the Museo Camilo Visedo Arqueológico, featuring Iberian treasures. The Museo de Fiestas de Moros y Cristianos (see **MUSEUMS**) is equally interesting. Take the N 340 back towards Alicante and turn right towards Bañeres. This pleasant wooded road is one of the richest botanical areas in the Province and in early summer its poppy fields are a riot of colour. Turn left off the C 3313 towards Ibi and after 3 km, right towards Onil.

93 km - Onil (see **CASTLES 1**). Visit the castle tucked away in the town centre, now occupied by council offices. Take the road left to Castalla.

97 km - Castalla (see **CASTLES 1**, **EXCURSION 3**). The ruined, inaccessible castle is an impressive landmark. See also the 14thC Ermita de la Sangre. Follow the road back to Alicante (36 km).

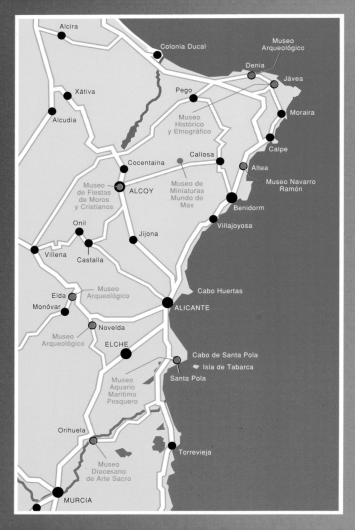

MUSEO DE FIESTAS DE MOROS Y CRISTIANOS
Casal de San Jordi, c/ San Miguel 60, Alcoy.
•1030-1300, 1630-2000 Mon.-Fri., 1630-2000 Sat. & Sun. •Free.
Background material to the fiesta. See **Fiestas**, **Moros y Cristianos**.

MUSEO NAVARRO RAMÓN Casa de Cultura, c/ Ibáñez, Altea.
•1030-1300, 1700-2000 Tues.-Sat., 1700-2000 Sun. •Free.
Small museum in a thriving artistic community.

MUSEO ARQUEOLÓGICO Castillo de Denia.
•0900-1330, 1700-2000. •Free.
Exhibits from the Moorish period and prehistoric and Roman times.

MUSEO ARQUEOLÓGICO Príncipe de Asturias 40, Elda.
•1000-1300, 1700-2000. •Free.
Archeological finds from the region.

MUSEO DE MINIATURAS MUNDO DE MAX Guadalest.
•1000-1900. Bus from Benidorm, Altea, Playa de Albir •200ptas
Vast collection of tiny paintings, sculptures and curiosities.

MUSEO HISTÓRICO Y ETNOGRÁFICO c/ Primicias 1, Jávea.
•1000-1300, 1700-2000 Tues.-Sun. •Free.
Small museum with exhibits on the history of the town.

MUSEO ARQUEOLÓGICO c/ Jaime II 3, Novelda.
•1900-2130. •Free.
Collection of interesting remnants of past times.

MUSEO DIOCESANO DE ARTE SACRO Catedral, Orihuela.
•1000-1330, 1730-1930 Mon.-Sat.
Includes The Temptation of St Thomas *said to be by Velázquez.*

MUSEO AQUARIO MARÍTIMO PESQUERO Santa Pola.
•1000-1330, 1700-2000 Tues.-Sun.
Collection of exhibits on a nautical theme.

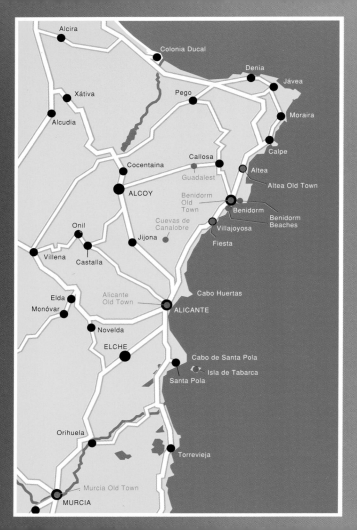

ALTEA OLD TOWN
Admire the charming hilltop square, the tiny blue-tiled parish church and the view of the Peñón de Ifach (see WALK 4, A-Z). See EXCURSION 1, A-Z.

ALICANTE OLD TOWN
Visit the Castillo de Santa Bárbara, the Iglesia de Santa María and the Museo de Arte del Siglo XX. See WALK 1, ALICANTE 2, A-Z.

BENIDORM BEACHES
If you like crowds visit the Playa de Levante, or for a quieter time try Mal Pas, Poniente or La Cala. See BEACHES 2, RESORT REVIEW 1, A-Z.

BENIDORM OLD TOWN
Ignore the 'Roast beef and Yorkshire pudding' restaurants and go native at the inexpensive tapas bars. See the pretty Balcón de Mer and try the Casa d'Andalucia instead of the Benidorm Palace (see BENIDORM 1). See A-Z.

CUEVAS DE CANALOBRE
As you descend into this cave, surrounded by eerily-lit shapes and dramatic music, you will feel as if you are in an alien world. See EXCURSION 4.

FIESTAS
Any Costa Blanca fiesta is worth seeing but try to catch Moros y Cristianos (see A-Z) or Las Hogueras de San Juan (see A-Z). See A-Z.

GUADALEST
One of the most spectacular places in Spain. The views from this once-impenetrable fortress are unrivalled on the Costa. See EXCURSION 2, A-Z.

ISLA DE TABARCA
A tiny, peaceful island community with interesting old buildings, a good beach and several coves. See A-Z.

MURCIA OLD TOWN
A splendid collection of interesting old buildings in an elegant setting. Don't miss the Casino and the Catedral. See WALK 2, WHAT TO SEE 2, A-Z.

Alicante

Murcia

Catedral, Murcia

Cuevas de Canalobre

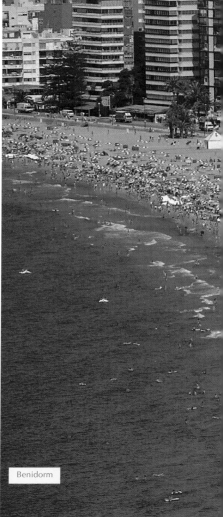
Benidorm

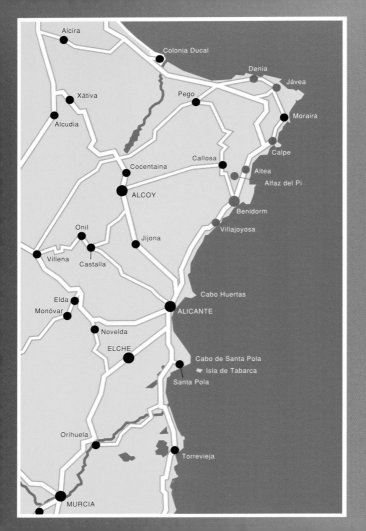

DENIA: pop 22,000. Alicante 100 km.
Good beaches, with the old town 10 min away. Ruined castle and superb views from Mount Mongó (see **WALK 3***). Many expatriate British, Germans, and Scandinavians. See* **BEACHES 1**, **EXCURSION 1**, **RESTAURANTS 2**, **A-Z**.

JÁVEA: pop 10,900. Alicante 92 km.
Small beaches with grottos and dramatic coves. Yachting centre and a lively resort. There is a Parador, fortified church and an interesting modern church shaped like a boat. See **BEACHES 1**, **EXCURSION 1**, **RESTAURANTS 3**, **A-Z**.

CALPE: pop 8000. Alicante 65 km.
Busy but pleasant resort with excellent beaches. The main feature is the rock of the Peñón de Ifach (see **WALK 4**, **A-Z***) - a tunnel and path lead to the summit. There are restaurants and bars in the town and a Mudéjar church. See* **BEACHES 2**, **EXCURSION 1**, **RESTAURANTS 1**, **A-Z**.

ALTEA: pop 11,200. Alicante 55 km.
A peaceful town of white houses set on cliffs above the sea. The church has a good example of a Valencian dome lined with blue tiles. The beach is not particularly good. Popular with French tourists. See **EXCURSION 1**, **A-Z**.

ALFAZ DEL PI: pop 5,800. Alicante 50 km.
The town name means 'Hamlet of Pines'. A small resort based on holiday chalets developments. There are beaches at El Albir (see **BEACHES 2***).

BENIDORM: pop 35,000. Alicante 42 km.
A very compact resort with a huge 6.4 km-long beach. The beach is lined with a Manhattan-like array of high-rise hotels and apartment blocks. This is a very popular resort for families and young people with a wide range of restaurants, good nightlife and, reflecting its popularity with the British, many English pubs. See **BEACHES 2**, **BENIDORM**, **A-Z**.

VILLAJOYOSA: pop 21,000. Alicante 30 km.
A fishing village with characteristic white houses. It is a minor resort with a colourful market and reputedly the best Moros y Cristianos festival (see **Fiestas**, **A-Z***) on the Costa. See* **BEACHES 3**, **A-Z**.

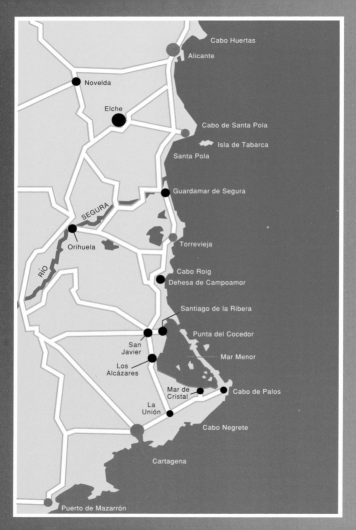

ALICANTE: pop 258,000. Benidorm 42 km.
The air gateway to the Costa Blanca and a thriving, bustling Spanish town, not just a tourist resort. There are beaches at Playa del Postiguet, and Playa de San Juan has a huge sandy beach and tall apartment blocks and hotels (see BEACHES 3). The city has many attractions including the Castillo de Santa Bárbara, the Iglesia Colegial de San Nicolás de Bari, the Museo de Arte del Siglo XX (Picasso, Miró, Dalí, etc), the Ayuntamiento (Town Hall) and a lively old quarter - Santa Cruz. See ALICANTE, WALK 1, A-Z.

SANTA POLA: pop 12,000. Alicante 20 km.
Good beaches (see BEACHES 4). There are boat trips to the Isla de Tabarca (see MUSTS, A-Z) and nearby is a necropolis with Iberian and Roman remains as well as saltpans with flamingoes (see Fauna). See A-Z.

TORREVIEJA: pop 12,300. Alicante 45 km.
Plenty of modern hotels on the cliffs above the old town and building is still going on in this developing area. There are very good beaches to the south (see BEACHES 4), and in the town itself, rapidly becoming an international resort, there are bars, restaurants and a lively nightlife scene.

MAR MENOR: Alicante 80 km.
A vast 170 km² lagoon with shallow, warm water. The beaches along the lagoon side are calmer and warmer than on the Mediterranean coast (see BEACHES 4). The stretch of coast dividing the lagoon from the sea is called La Manga (the sleeve) and this is where most development takes place. The urbanizaciones (see A-Z) are mainly at the southern end of La Manga. This area offers a vast range of water sports facilities. See A-Z.

CARTAGENA: pop 170,000. Alicante 115 km.
An important industrial and naval port dominated by the historic arsenal (1782). The old town spreads out around the ruined 13thC cathedral. There is a nudist beach at El Portus and a fine beach at Cabo de Palos. See A-Z.

PUERTO DE MAZARRÓN: pop 10,000. Alicante 145 km.
A pleasant resort with sandy beaches lying along a vast bay. There is an old fishing harbour and the development is based on second homes in the hills.

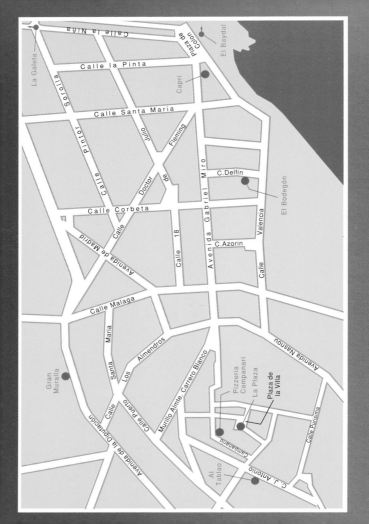

Calpe

AL TABLAO c/ José Antonio.
•Budget-Moderate.
Attractive bar and restaurant serving mainly snacks. There is a flamenco show (see **A-Z***) every Saturday at 2230.*

CAPRI Av Gabriel Miró.
•Expensive.
Popular restaurant overlooking the beach. Spanish and regional specialities. Renowned for its fish cooked in salt crust and for an excellent wine cellar.

EL BAYDAL Av del Puerto (the fishing harbour).
•Moderate.
Calpe's best restaurant for fresh seafood. Other local dishes are also on offer here and you can eat inside or out on the terrace.

EL BODEGÓN Edfo Damarac, c/ Delfín.
•Moderate-Expensive.
Typical Spanish restaurant serving local and international dishes on a charming terrace. Excellent paella *(see* **Food***).*

GRAN MURALLA Av de la Diputación.
•Moderate.
Chinese restaurant serving Pekinese, Cantonese and Indonesian dishes.

LA GALETA Partida la Calalga, northern end of Playa de Levante.
•Expensive.
Classic restaurant of a large hotel at the beach. International cuisine.

PIZZERIA CAMPANARI c/ Campanario.
•Evenings only. •Budget.
Pizza specialities plus other Italian dishes in a quiet corner of the old town beneath the church bell-tower.

LA PLAZA Plaza de la Villa.
•Evenings only. •Budget-Moderate.
Lively small restaurant serving salads, grilled fish and paella *(see* **Food***).*

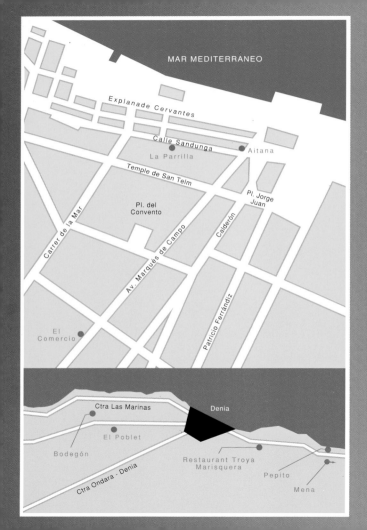

Denia

AITANA c/ Sandunga and Av Marqués de Campo.
•Moderate.
*Small restaurant above a bar. Extensive menu ranging from inexpensive
platos combinados (see **Food**) to excellent rice and seafood specialities.*

BODEGÓN Urb La Felicidad, Ctra Las Marinas.
•Expensive.
Fine gourmet cuisine in a rustic setting.

EL COMERCIO Av Marqués de Campo.
•Budget.
*German restaurant and beer garden serving delicious tapas (see **A-Z**).
Enjoy the music and dancing on the patio in summer.*

EL POBLET Urb El Poblet, Ctra Las Marinas.
•Expensive.
Pretty restaurant hidden from road by bougainvillea. International cuisine.

LA PARRILLA c/ Sandunga.
•Moderate.
*Good French and Spanish dishes served in a bodega-style restaurant with an
attractive summer patio.*

MENA End of the road to Playa las Rotas.
•Moderate.
*Large restaurant on the edge of the sea offering excellent local cuisine plus
some international dishes. The terrace has fine views.*

PEPITO Road to Playa las Rotas (next to Mesón Rotas).
•Fri.-Wed. •Moderate.
Typical Spanish restaurant with pleasant rustic atmosphere. Friendly service.

RESTAURANT TROYA MARISQUERA Playa las Rotas.
•Expensive.
*Large and popular restaurant in a modern complex serving Arroz a banda
(see **Food**) and grilled fish specialities. Eat inside or on the terrace.*

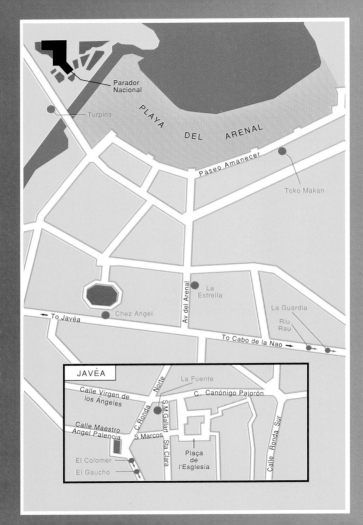

Jávea

CHEZ ANGEL Ctra Cabo de la Nao, Playa del Arenal.
• Wed.-Mon. • Expensive.
*Traditional tapas (see **Food**), and excellent French and Spanish food.*

EL COLOMER Ctra Jávea, Jesús Pobre.
• Budget.
'The art of grilling and barbecuing meat the South American way' they say.

EL GAUCHO Ctra Jávea, Jesús Pobre.
• Open evenings only in summer. • Moderate-Expensive.
Churrasquearía (barbecue restaurant). Grilled meats South American style.

LA ESTRELLA Av del Arenal.
• Expensive.
Small and attractive French/international restaurant.

LA FUENTE c/ Sor María Gallart.
• Evenings only. • Expensive.
Interesting international menu in this 17thC building in the old town.

LA GUARDIA Urb Costa Nova (road to Playa de Granadella).
• Expensive.
Classy spot in the woods of Cabo de la Nao. French and Spanish dishes.

RIU RAU Costa Nova Panorama.
• Moderate-Expensive.
Traditional Alicantino meals in a very pretty hillside setting.

TURPINS Playa del Arenal (opposite Parador Nacional).
• Open evenings only. • Moderate.
Small, inviting restaurant with a summer terrace. Fine international cuisine.

TOKO MAKAN Playa del Arenal.
• Moderate.
Excellent Rijstafel (15-20 different dishes) served by friendly Dutch owners in this Indonesian-style beach restaurant.

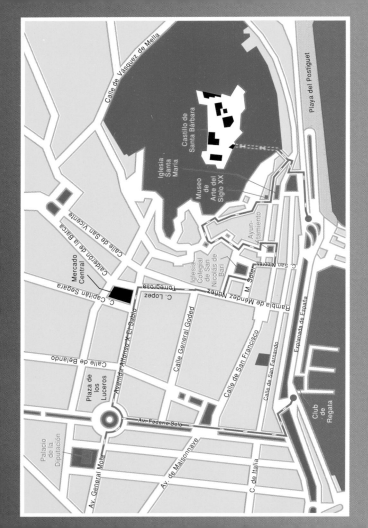

Alicante

Start from the fountains at the east end of the Explanada de España. Heading further east, stay on the left hand side of the street, across from the beach, and enter the tunnel which leads to the lift up to the Castillo de Santa Bárbara (see **ALICANTE 2**). Walk around its three levels, the first dating from the early 18thC Bourbon époque, the second from the 16thC and at the top the original fortress some 166 m above sea level, mostly built in the 13thC. Explore inside the castle, visit the fiesta museum, Museo de las Hogueras de San Juan (see **ALICANTE 2**), and enjoy the splendid views.

Take the lift down and walk back up Fray Juan Rico to the beautiful 14thC Iglesia Santa María, one of Spain's finest medieval Christian churches (see **ALICANTE 2**). Next to the church is the Alicante region's best collection of modern art in the Museo de Arte del Siglo XX (see **ALICANTE 2**). Turn right out of the Plaza Santa María and explore the oldest part of Alicante, the Barrio de Santa Cruz (*barrio* meaning 'quarter'), which includes the Calle Labradores, a very narrow street of bars and houses, complete with their original Baroque facades and ancient wrought iron balconies.

Make your way to the Ayuntamiento (Town Hall) via the Calle San Agustín. Admire the splendid 18thC facade of the town hall and, if possible, visit inside (see **ALICANTE 2**). From the Plaza del Ayuntamiento take the Calle Rafael Altamira, turn right into Calle San Nicolás and left into Miguel Soler where you will find the entrance to the 17thC Iglesia Colegial de San Nicolás de Bari (also referred to locally as a cathedral) on the right (see **ALICANTE 2**). Admire the church's Baroque facade and inside, visit the splendid 18thC Chapel de la Comunión. Turn right out of the church then left into Alicante's main shopping and commercial street, the Rambla de Méndez Núñez. Turn right and continue until it forks to the left into the Calle López Torregrosa. Turn left into the Avenida Alfonso X El Sabio. Go past the Mercado Central (market), on your right, and continue to the Plaza de los Luceros. Cross this island and on the right is the Palacio de la Diputación - the Council Hall of the Province of Alicante. This contains the Museo Arqueológico Provincial (see **ALICANTE 2**). Return to the Plaza de los Luceros and turn right down Avenida Federic Solo, leading down to the port and the colourful Club de Regata and rejoining the Explanada de España.

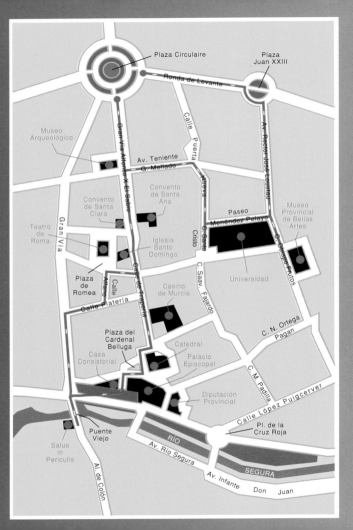

Murcia

Start at the Plaza Circulaire where there is an excellent water fountain display at certain times of day. Go down the Ronda de Levante and turn right at the Plaza Juan XXIII into the Avenida Rector José Loustau. Shortly, this becomes the Calle Obispo Frutos. On the left is the Museo Provincial de Bellas Artes (see **WHAT TO SEE 2**). Backtrack and then turn second left into Paseo Menéndez Pelayo. Standing on the left is the Universidad, formerly a monastery for La Merced monks, which still boasts a fine Baroque facade which can be seen if you walk around the building and turn left into the Calle Santo Cristo. Turn around and walk up the Calle Puerta Nueva then left into Avenida Teniente G. Mellado. On the other side of the Gran Vía Alfonso X El Sabio stands the Museo Arqueológico (see **WHAT TO SEE 2**).

Walk down the Gran Vía Alfonso X and on your right is the Convento de Santa Clara, dating from the 12thC. Opposite is the Convento de Santa Ana, also 12thC and, like Santa Clara, rebuilt in the 17thC. Continue along the road and on your right is the lovely 17thC Iglesia Santo Domingo. At this point the Gran Vía Alfonso X becomes the pedestrianized Calle de Trapería. On the left is the splendid Casino de Murcia. No longer a gaming casino, it is a fascinating building open to the public (see **WHAT TO SEE 2**). Continue further down the street to the magnificent Catedral, which dates from the 14thC. Its splendid Baroque decorations were added in 1737. After visiting the Catedral and its museum (see **WHAT TO SEE 2**) walk to the right of the Catedral into Plaza del Cardenal Belluga and admire the view of the Catedral from this side, as well as the statue of the Cardinal - a powerful 18thC Murcian prelate. The early 18thC Palacio Episcopal (Bishop's Palace) stands on the Plaza flanked on the left by the Diputación Provincial and on the right by the 19thC Casa Consistorial (the Town Hall). Walk between these buildings to view them from the front and you will find yourself next to the river. Cross the 18thC Puente Viejo (Old Bridge) and have a look at the similarly ancient chapel inscribed *Salus in Periculis*, dedicated to Murcian flood victims. Walk back up Murcia's second Gran Vía and turn right into Calle Platería. Take the third left into Calle Alfano which leads to the Plaza de Romea and its lovely pink and grey 18thC theatre, Teatro de Roma. Turn right to rejoin the Gran Vía Alfonso X and left back to the Plaza Circulaire.

Casino, Murcia

Murcia

Aitana

Rural

WALK 3 - MONTE MONGÓ: 2 hr 30 min.

An impressive mountain dominating the coastline between Denia (see **RESORT REVIEW 1**, **A-Z**) and Jávea (see **RESORT REVIEW 1**, **A-Z**). Start from the coast road linking the towns and follow the footpath as it winds up towards the 750 m summit. The walk is fairly strenuous and not to be undertaken lightly, but the view is a splendid reward for your exertions.

WALK 4 - PEÑÓN DE IFACH: 1 hr 30 min.

A large rock similar to Gibraltar and the most outstanding landmark on the Costa Blanca. The way to the foot of the Peñón de Ifach (see **A-Z**) is well signposted from Calpe (see **RESORT REVIEW 1**, **A-Z**). Once there, take care not to follow the more direct-looking path, as that route is very taxing. Half an hour's steady walking on the other track should be enough to take you to the top, and the views are really exhilarating.

WALK 5 - SIERRA HELADA: 5 hr.

This hike takes you from Benidorm (see **RESORT REVIEW 1**, **A-Z**) to the Playa de Albir (see **BEACHES 2**) and Altea (see **RESORT REVIEW 1**, **A-Z**) by the most pleasant route, if not the shortest. The starting point, in the Rincón de Loix (east part of Benidorm), is well signposted and easy to find. Follow the footpath to the sea and along the cliffs to Albir. Some scrambling is required, but nothing exhausting or dangerous, and there are many bars and cafés in Altea to refresh you when you get there.

WALK 6 - AITANA: 4 hr.

The village of Alcolecha is situated close to this mountain, off the Ctra Callosa de Ensarriá-Alcoy (turn off at Benasau). Just south of Alcolecha there is a military base, and a few hundred metres further on there is a track leading to the picnic area of Font del Abre. Park at this site. The footpath begins on the right, where the track turns sharp left. Head coastwards for about 30 min to below the TV transmitter complex. When you come to the scree, walk across it, always heading east (don't attempt to climb up at this point). After the scree, search on your right for the rather poorly-defined path to the summit, and scramble your way up through the gap in the rock. The path takes you past the Simas de Partagas, large and very deep fissures. Return by the same route.

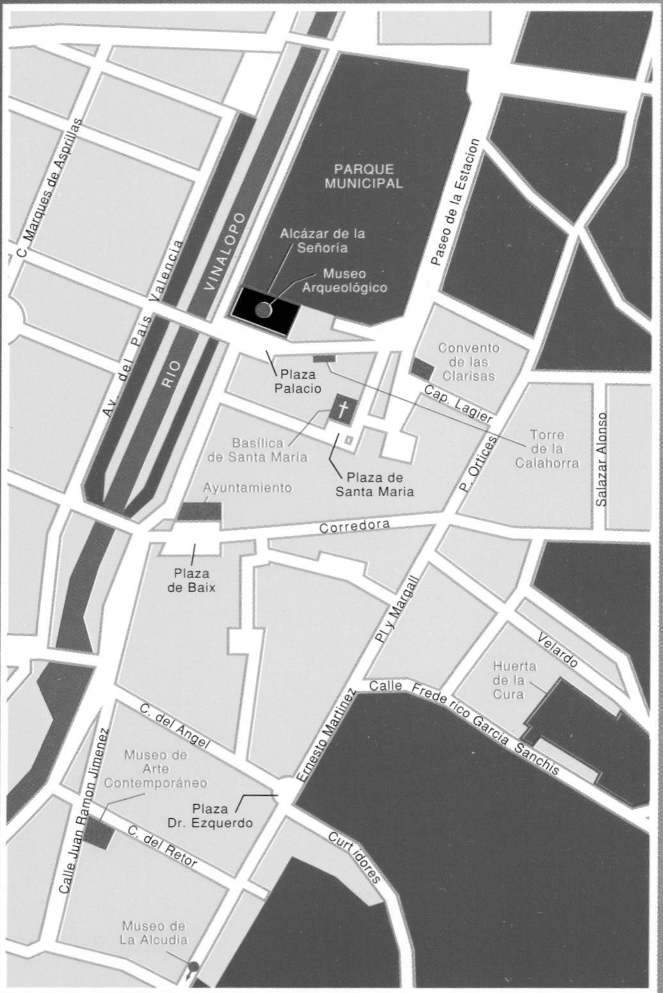
PARQUE MUNICIPAL
Alcázar de la Señoría
Museo Arqueológico
Paseo de la Estacion
C. Marques de Asprillas
Av. del Pais Valencia
RIO VINALOPO
Plaza Palacio
Convento de las Clarisas
Cap. Lagier
Torre de la Calahorra
Salazar Alonso
P. Ortices
Basílica de Santa María
Plaza de Santa Maria
Ayuntamiento
Corredora
Plaza de Baix
Pi y Margall
Velardo
Huerta de la Cura
Calle Frede rico Garcia Sanchis
Ernesto Martinez
C. del Angel
Calle Juan Ramon Jimenez
Museo de Arte Contemporáneo
Plaza Dr. Ezquerdo
C. del Retor
Curt idores
Museo de La Alcudia

Elche

ALCÁZAR DE LA SEÑORÍA Plaza Palacio.
• Admission to Museo Arqueológico only (see below).
The 15thC Moorish 'Palace of the Lord', once part of the city wall.

AYUNTAMIENTO Plaza de Baix.
• No admission.
Well-preserved 15thC town hall with original doors and 17thC clock tower.

BASÍLICA (IGLESIA) DE SANTA MARÍA Plaza de Santa María.
• 0900-1300, 1700-2000.
*Huge 17thC church, the venue for the Misterio de Elche (see **A-Z**).*

CONVENTO DE LAS CLARISAS (LA MERCED) Cap. Lagier.
• Admission during services only.
The small modern chapel is the only accessible part of the convent.

HUERTA (HORT) DE LA CURA c/ Federico García Sanchis.
• 0900-2030 Tues.-Sat. • 200ptas, child 100ptas.
*The 'Priest's Grove' is a nationally famous collection of palms, cacti, flowers and monuments, including a replica of La Dama de Elche (see **A-Z**).*

MUSEO ARQUEOLÓGICO Alcázar de la Señoría (see above).
• 1000-1300 Mon., 1000-1300, 1600-1900 Tues.-Sun. • 50ptas.
Collection of local finds including prehistoric, Iberian and Greek remains.

MUSEO DE ARTE CONTEMPORÁNEO c/ Juan Ramón Jiménez.
• 1000-1300 Sun., 1000-1300, 1600-1900 Tues.-Fri. • 50ptas, free Sat.
Contemporary Spanish art, housed in Elche's old Moorish town hall.

TORRE DE LA CALAHORRA Plaza Palacio.
• 1700-2000 Mon.-Fri. • Free (admission to Galería de Arte only).
Fortress tower constructed by the Moors in the 14thC. Houses an art gallery.

MUSEO DE LA ALCUDIA Alcudia, 2 km south of Elche.
• 0900-2000 Tues.-Sun. • 50ptas.
Over 3000 exhibits relating to this ancient site. Excavations open to view.

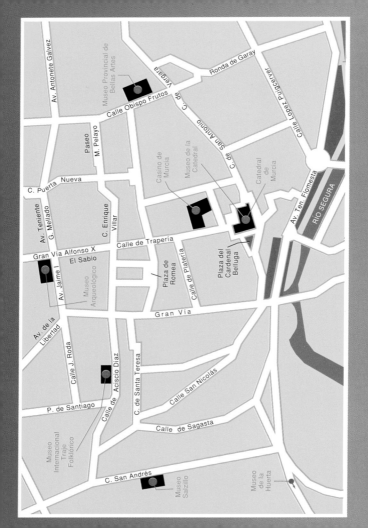

MUSEO PROVINCIAL DE BELLAS ARTES c/ Obispo Frutos.
•0900-1400, 1700-1900 Tues.-Sun., 1100-1400 hols. •75ptas.
Excellent and varied collection of Spanish paintings and sculpture on three floors, ranging from the 15th-20thC. See **WALK 2**.

MUSEO ARQUEOLÓGICO c/ Gran Vía Alfonso X El Sabio.
•0900-1400, 1700-2000 Tues.-Sat., 1100-1400 Sun. & hols. •75ptas.
Display of 17th-18thC Hispano-Moresque ceramics and glass. See **WALK 2**.

CASINO DE MURCIA c/ de Trapería.
Guided tour by steward, no charge but tip is normal.
Former 19thC gaming house with Mudéjar *entrance, Louis XV-style rooms, ballroom, chess and billiards rooms. See* **WALK 2**.

CATEDRAL DE MURCIA Plaza del Cardenal Belluga.
•1000-1300, 1700-2000.
The most splendid building in the province (built 14thC). Admire the Capilla de los Vélez, Capilla Mayor, the sacristy and the fantastic view. See **WALK 2**.

MUSEO DE LA HUERTA Alcantarilla, 7 km from Murcia.
•0900-1300, 1600-1800 Tues.-Sat., 1000-1400 Sun.
An ethnological and agricultural museum of the Murcian countryside.

MUSEO DE LA CATEDRAL Plaza del Cardenal Belluga.
•1000-1300, 1700-2000. •100ptas.
Magnificent church treasures, dating back to the 14thC - plate, altar pieces, art and sculptures, including Saint Hieronymous *by Salzillo. See* **WALK 2**.

MUSEO SALZILLO c/ San Andrés.
•0930-1300, 1600-1900 Apr.-Sept., 0930-1300, 1500-1800 Oct.-Mar., 1000-1300 hols. •100ptas.
Sculptures by Murcia's most famous son, Francisco Salzillo.

MUSEO INTERNACIONAL TRAJE FOLKLÓRICO c/ A. Díaz.
•1000-1330, 1700-2000 Tues.-Sat., 1000-1300 Sun. •100ptas.
Collection of local costumes and information on traditions and folklore.

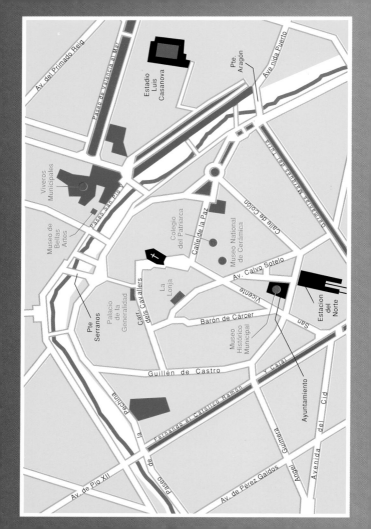

COLEGIO DEL PATRIARCA Ctra de la Nave 1.
•1100-1300 Sat., Sun. & hols.
Contains El Greco's beautiful painting The Adoration of the Shepherds.

LA LONJA Mercado Central, Plaza del Mercado.
•0900-1300, 1600-1800 Sat., 1000-1300 Sun.
Old silk market, in Gothic style, close to the Iglesia de Santos Juanes.

MUSEO DE BELLAS ARTES Paseo San Pio V.
•1000-1400, 1600-1800 Mon.-Sat., 1000-1400 Sun. & hols.
Paintings by Velázquez, El Greco, Van Dyck, Ribera, and others. Located in a splendid old seminary (1683) built around a quiet and shady patio.

MUSEO DE FALLAS Plaza de Monteolivete 4.
•1000-1400, 1600-1900 Tues.-Sun.
Collection of huge satirical statues made in wood and papier-mâché normally burnt in the closing ceremony at the end of the fiesta.

MUSEO HISTÓRICO MUNICIPAL Ayuntamiento,
Plaza del País Valenciano 1.
•0900-1300 Mon.-Fri.
Very interesting for historians. Fascinating old maps.

MUSEO NATIONAL DE CERÁMICA Rinconada de García
Sanchis (access from Plaza de Zaragoza).
•1000-1400, 1600-1800 Tues.-Sat., 1000-1400 Sun.
Located in the Palacio del Marqués Dos Aguas , built in the 15thC with a magnificent Baroque facade. All about pottery and handicrafts.

PALACIO DE LA GENERALIDAD Carrer dels Cavallers
•0930-1300, 1530-2000 Fri.-Wed.
Beautiful Gothic style with exceptional patio erected from 1481 to 1510.

VIVEROS MUNICIPALES Paseo San Pio V.
•0900-1930. Closed on wet days.
Gardens presenting the flora of the country in a beautiful setting.

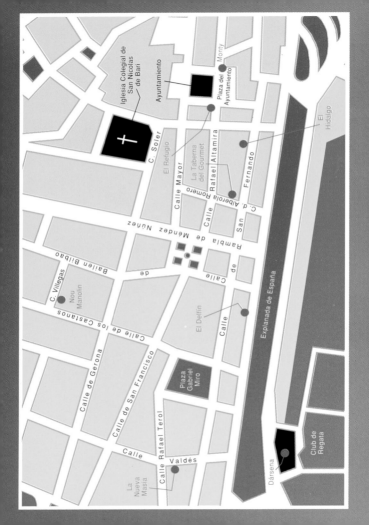

Restaurants

DÁRSENA Club de Regata, Explanada de España.
•Tues.-Sun. •Expensive.
Modern restaurant with good views of the harbour. Rice and fish specialities including a local version of bouillabaisse.

EL DELFÍN Explanada de España 12.
•Expensive.
Reputedly the best in Alicante (1 star in 1988 Michelin Guide). Seafood and international cuisine. Luxurious setting. Cocktail bar/café downstairs.

EL HIDALGO c/ de San Fernando.
•Moderate.
International and Spanish dishes in a typical Alicantino restaurant

MONTY Plaza del Ayuntamiento.
•Moderate.
Spanish and international food. You can eat in the more formal dining area or relax on the terrace on the town square.

NOU MANOLIN c/ Villegas.
•Expensive.
*Up-market tapas bar (see **A-Z**). The restaurant serves Alicantino specialities.*

LA NUEVA MASIA c/ Valdés.
•Mon.-Sat. •Moderate.
*Good tapas (see **A-Z**) and Spanish/international food with rice and fish specialities are served in high-class 'rustic' surroundings.*

LA TABERNA DEL GOURMET c/ de Alberola Romero.
•Moderate.
*Top quality tapas bar (see **A-Z**) and restaurant - popular at lunchtimes.*

EL REFUGIO Plaza del Ayuntamiento.
•Inexpensive-Moderate.
Friendly family-run restaurant serving Spanish dishes with the emphasis on fish. Eat inside or on the outside terrace.

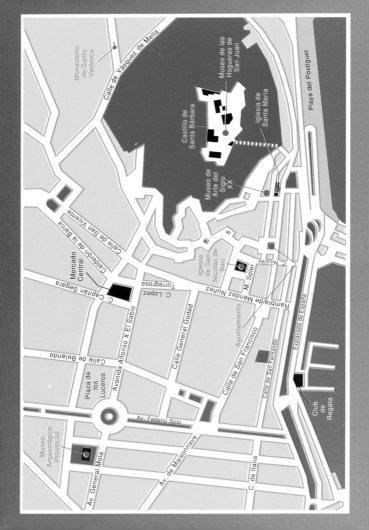

What to See

CASTILLO DE SANTA BÁRBARA
•0900-1900 Oct.-Mar., 0900-2000 Apr.-May, 0900-2100 June-Sept.
Closed 1400 Sat. •Lift 75ptas. Castle free.
13th-16thC structure with a prison cell and chapel. See WALK 1.

MUSEO DE LAS HOGUERAS DE SAN JUAN
Castillo de Santa Bárbara.
•1000-1300, 1700-1900 Sun.-Fri., 1000-1300 Sat. •25ptas.
Colourful collection of fiesta figures. See WALK 1, **Hogueras de San Juan**.

IGLESIA DE SANTA MARÍA Plaza Santa María.
•Open during services.
Built in the 14thC but famous for its 18thC Baroque facade. See WALK 1.

MUSEO DE ARTE DEL SIGLO XX Plaza Santa María.
•1000-1300, 1700-2000 Tues.-Sat., 1000-1300 Sun. (Oct.-Apr.);
1030-1330, 1800-2100 Tues.-Sat., 1030-1330 Sun. (May-Sept.). •Free.
*Modern gallery in Alicante's oldest domestic building (1685). Exhibits works
by Dalí, Picasso, Miró and Chagall, among others. See* WALK 1.

IGLESIA COLEGIAL DE SAN NICOLÁS DE BARI c/ Nicolás.
•1000-1230, 1800-2030 Mon.-Fri., 0900-1345 Sat.-Sun.
Splendid church with ornate Baroque facade, nave and altar. See WALK 1.

MUSEO ARQUEOLÓGICO PROVINCIAL Av General Mola 6.
•0930-1330 Mon.-Fri. •Free.
Iberian, Carthaginian, Greek and Moorish finds from the area. See WALK 1.

AYUNTAMIENTO Plaza del Ayuntamiento.
•0900-1500 Mon.-Fri. •Free.
A picture gallery and chapel are among the public rooms. See WALK 1.

MONASTERIO DE SANTA VERÓNICA Ctra Alicante-Valencia.
•1000-1300, 1700-2000 Mon.- Fri.
*Built on the site where, during a procession, a tear appeared on the holy
cloth believed to have mopped Christ's brow at Calvary. See* EXCURSION 4.

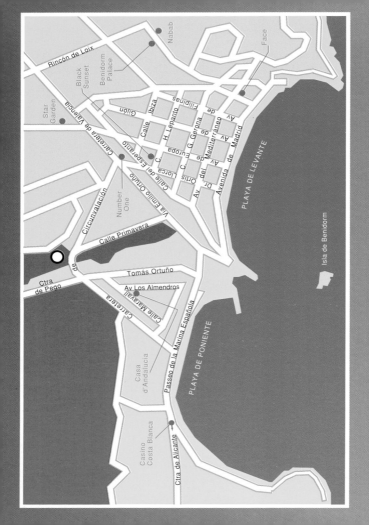

BENIDORM PALACE, c/ de la Diputación, Rincón de Loix.
•2130 Tues.-Sat. •2400ptas.
International cabaret, music and dance spectaculars including a flamenco ballet (see A-Z). Seats for 2200 people and one of the world's largest stages.

CASINO COSTA BLANCA Ctra Alicante-Valencia, 5 km from Benidorm towards Villajoyosa.
•2000-0400. •1500ptas.
Blackjack, French and American roulette, slot machines, etc. Cash only at the tables. Minimum age 21, passport and smart dress compulsory.

CASA D'ANDALUCIA c/ Maravall.
•Show 2200-0400. •Entry free, but drinks expensive.
Popular flamenco bar (see A-Z), with live shows daily.

STAR GARDEN Ctra Alicante-Valencia, signposted km 122.
•2200-0800. •2000ptas.
Large discotheque for the more sophisticated crowd with swimming pool, outdoor dance floors and lasers. Dramatic setting.

NABAB Rincón de Loix.
•2200-0800. •1500ptas.
One of the most famous night spots on the Costa Blanca. It has an exclusive atmosphere with open-air dance floors and lasers.

NUMBER ONE Ctra de Circunvalación s/n.
•2230-0500. •1000ptas.
Large trendy disco with a very Spanish ambience, attracting a younger set.

FACE Av del Mediterráneo.
•2100-0400. •Free.
Disco newly refurbished in summer 1989. Young crowd, laser lightshow.

BLACK SUNSET c/ de Lepanto s/n.
•2200-0800. •Entry free, but drinks very expensive.
More of a nightclub than a disco. Popular with the older generations.

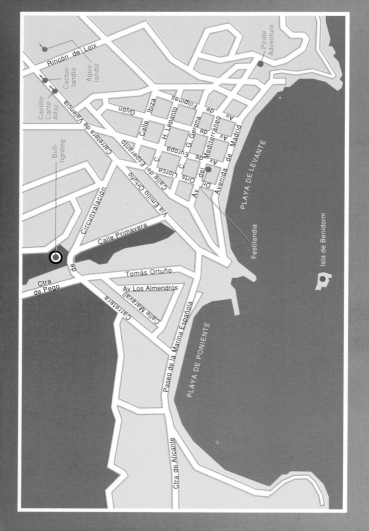

Recreation

AQUALANDIA Partida de Bayo s/n, Sierra Helada.
•1000-2200. Bus 4, 6 or Aqualand Express from Pza Triangular.
•1400ptas, child 700ptas.
This well-equipped aqua-park comprises water-chutes, water toboggans, rapids, falls and swimming pools. Good supervision by a large staff.

BULLFIGHTING Plaza de Toros, Benidorm.
•Alternative Sundays. •1000ptas (*sombre*), 700ptas (*sol*).
Between June and October budding matadors take part in novice bullfights which do not involve killing the bull. See **A-Z**.

CACTUSLANDIA La Galera del Mar 27, Altea.
Ctra Valencia-Alicante, between Altea and Calpe.
•0900-2000. •300 ptas, child 150 ptas.
More than 1500 species of cacti, sub-tropical fruit trees and flowers on a terrace overlooking the sea. Includes Avelandia, a small bird collection.

CASTILLO CANTE ALFAZ Alfaz del Pi, 7 km from Benidorm,
•2000 Tues. & Thurs. •2900ptas, child 1450ptas (inc. food and drink).
A lively barbecue and disco evening.

FESTILANDIA Av del Mediterráneo, Benidorm.
•1000-1900 daily in summer.
Children's amusement park just off Playa de Levante (see **BEACHES 2***).*

ISLA DE BENIDORM
•Sailings depart from the port 1000-1700 on the hour.
•Return ticket 450ptas, child 350ptas.
A small uninhabited island with wild peacocks (see **Fauna***). Small beaches, good for diving and snorkelling.*

PIRATE ADVENTURE Tropicana Gardens Hotel,
Av Diputación, Benidorm.
•1845 Sun.-Mon. (July-Aug.), 1845 Mon. only (Sept.-June).
•2700ptas, child 1400ptas (inc. food and drink).
'A pirate feast amidst swashbuckling action' is promised here.

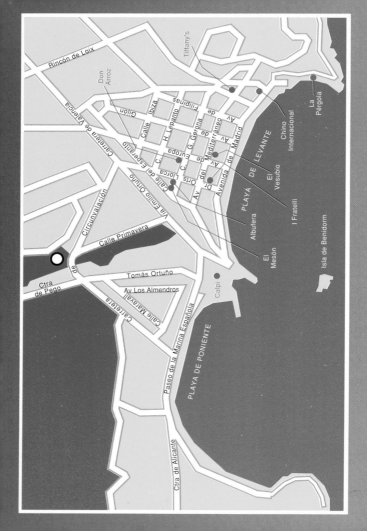

Restaurants

ALBUFERA c/ de Gerona, Av del Doctor Orts Llorca.
•Moderate (set menu 1000-2750ptas inc. wine).
Modern restaurant with French/international dishes and Spanish á la carte.

CALPI Plaza de la Constitución.
•Budget.
*Traditional tapas bar (see **A-Z**) with few frills, in the old town.*

CHINO INTERNACIONAL Av Ametilla de Mar.
•Moderate (set menus 725/925/1125ptas; set meal for two 2495ptas).
Some of the best Chinese food on the Costa. Á la carte also available.

DON ARROZ Av de Europa and c/ de Gerona.
Tues.-Sun. •Expensive.
*Smart, modern restaurant serving paella (see **Food**) and other rice dishes.*

EL MESÓN c/ Gerona and c/ Esperanto.
•Moderate.
*Restaurant and tapas bar (see **A-Z**) in traditional rustic setting.*

EL VESUBIO Av del Mediterráneo s/n.
•Budget.
Homemade pastas and pizzas are served at this modern Italian restaurant.

I FRATELLI Av del Doctor Orts Llorca 21.
•Expensive.
Excellent Italian food with fresh pasta specialities. Intimate atmosphere.

LA PÉRGOLA c/ Venticico, Rincón de Loix.
•Expensive.
In a splendid location with a terrace overlooking Playa de Levante (see BEACHES 2). International cuisine. Ideal for a special romantic evening.

TIFFANY'S Edfo Coblanca III, Av del Mediterráneo.
•Dinner only. •Expensive.
Interesting international menu and live piano music in elegant surroundings.

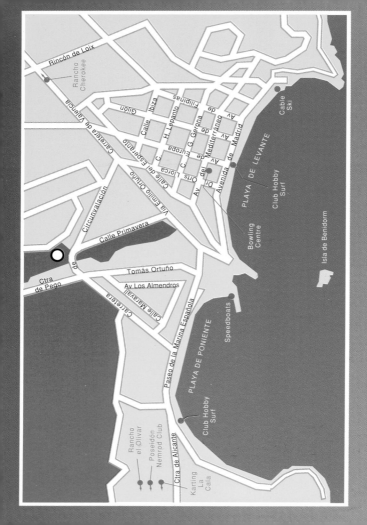

Sports

KARTING LA CALA Ctra Alicante-Valencia, 1 km from Benidorm.
•1100-2200. •700ptas (5 laps), 1100ptas (12 laps), 1300ptas (20 laps);
child 250ptas (5 laps), 400ptas (12 laps), 550ptas (20 laps).
Experience all the thrills of go-karting.

RANCHO CHEROKEE
Camino Viejo de Altea, 5 km from Benidorm.
•1000-1900. •700ptas per hr.
*Horse riding instruction, treks and classes in breaking in wild horses. There
are 20 horses of various breeds - Arabic, Spanish, Anglo-Arabic.*

RANCHO EL OLIVAR Av de la Marina.
•1000-1900. •700ptas per hr.
*Smaller horse riding club, with about nine horses. Full instruction is given
for beginners.*

POSEIDÓN NEMROD CLUB c/ Alfaz s/n, La Cala.
•0900-1900 May-Oct. •£50 per day (beginner's course £150 per wk).
Equipment hire for advanced scuba-divers and lessons for beginners.

SPEEDBOATS Hire from most ports.
•3500ptas per half hour (50 hp).•4000ptas per half hour (80 hp).
Prices include fuel, insurance and with the 80 hp boats, skis and instruction.

BOWLING CENTRE Av de Mediterráneo s/n.
•1100-1500, •300ptas per game; •1500-0200, •350ptas per game.
Ten-pin bowling alley of a high standard, with ten lanes.

CABLE SKI Av Rincón de Loix, Playa de Levante.
•1030-1900. •4 starts 1000ptas, 10 starts 2000ptas, 20 starts 3000ptas.
Water-skiing on a mechanical overhead cable-pull course.

CLUB HOBBY SURF Playa de Poniente and Playa de Levante.
•900ptas per hr (board hire), 8600ptas per six hr (tuition).
*Windsurfing equipment for hire. Lessons are available for those learning this
increasingly popular sport.*

Accidents and Breakdowns: If you are involved in a motoring accident, follow the normal procedure of exchanging insurance details, names and addresses with the other party. Try to establish witnesses' details also. If someone is injured call the police (see **Emergencies, A-Z**). If you are driving your own car you will need a bail bond from your insurance company to exempt you from having to spend time in police custody while awaiting the outcome of any enquiry.
Breakdowns: There are SOS points every 5 km on the main roads. Dial 091 for emergencies. The Real Automóvil Club de España (RACE) will provide you with a free towing service and mechanical assistance in case of accident or breakdown. Temporary membership is inexpensive and well worthwhile. Their address is Calle Orense 3, Alicante. Tel: (965) 22 93 49 or 22 98 61. See **Driving**.

Accommodation: There is a variety of accommodation available all over the Costa Blanca and prices are generally reasonable. Most places will have vacancies outside the high summer season, but between June and September booking in advance is recommended.
Apartments - generally one week minimum rent required.
Hotels - The grading system goes from 1-star to 5-star. A double room for one night costs around 3000-5000ptas in a 1- or 2-star hotel, 6000-10,000ptas in a 4-star hotel and upward of 12,000ptas for the best 5-star treatment. A *hotel residencial* (HR) is a hotel without its own dining room but not necessarily offering a lower standard of comfort. A *hostal* is a hotel of modest quality, usually costing about the same as a hotel with one less star. When checking in you must hand over your passport at the reception desk to get the room key.
Fondas - Traditional village inns where you can usually expect good local food and friendly service.
Paradores Nacionales - State-owned hotels which offer a high standard of accommodation. There are two on the Costa Blanca, at Jávea (see **EXCURSION 1, RESORT REVIEW 1, A-Z**) and Elche (see **A-Z**).
Pensiones - Cheap and basic guest houses.
Residencias - Rooms with a small kitchen (self-catering) and the same regulations as hotels.
See also **Camping and Caravanning, Tourist Information**.

Airport: The main airport in the Costa Blanca is El Altet, 10 km from Alicante and 52 km from Benidorm. It handles both domestic and international flights. The facilities include tourist office, bank, post office, telephones, bookshops (selling foreign as well as local newspapers), excellent duty-free shops with a large range of merchandise (and much lower prices than in local shops, particularly for alcoholic drinks), restaurants, bars and car hire agencies (*Avis* and *Hertz*). For information, tel: 28 50 11 or 21 85 10. For reservations, tel: 20 60 00.

Alcoy: Pop. 66,000. 57 km north of Alicante, 55 km west of Benidorm. An inland industrial town with a few features of interest, including the 18thC Iglesia de Santa María, the Plaza España and the Museo Camilo Visedo Arqueológico. Alcoy is the centre for the manufacture of *peladillas* (see **Food**), and is also notable for its spectacular annual *Moros y Cristianos* fiesta (see **A-Z**), 22-24 April. Mock battles, parades, pageants and fireworks set the town ablaze with excitement. The Museo de Fiestas de Moros y Cristianos in the Casal de San Jordi gives an insight into this fiesta (see **MUSEUMS**). See **EXCURSION 4**.

Alicante: Pop. 258,000. 42 km south west of Benidorm. Capital of the province. Founded by the Greeks and successively occupied by the Carthaginians and the Romans, who named it *Lucentum*, the City of Light. The older parts of the city, particularly around the Barrio de Santa Cruz, are most atmospheric at night when this cosmopolitan city comes to life. Young trendy Spaniards throng the streets and *tapas* bars (see **A-Z**) around the Rambla Méndez Núñez whilst the presence of US service personnel on shore leave helps create the slightly seedy (though safe) atmosphere, typical of a bustling Mediterranean port. By day there are architectural treasures to admire, including the towering fortress of Santa Bárbara, the Renaissance-style cloisters of the Gothic Iglesia Colegial de San Nicholás de Bari, and Baroque buildings such

as the Ayuntamiento (Town Hall) and the Iglesia de Santa María. The modern paintings in the Museo de Arte del Siglo XX constitute the finest collection in this part of Spain. See also the elegant shops in the Calle Mayor and the Ramblas Méndez Núñez and walk the famous promenade of the Explanada de España. Alicante stages many excellent fiestas (see **MUSTS, A-Z**), the most outstanding being the Hogueras de San Juan (see **A-Z**). There are many excellent beaches in the vicinity (see **BEACHES 3**) and excursions to the Isla de Tabarca (see **MUSTS, A-Z**) are popular. See **RESORT REVIEW 2, WALK 1, ALICANTE**.

Altea: Pop. 11,200. 55 km north east of Alicante, 11 km north east of Benidorm. The old quarter of this picturesque town, sitting high on a hill, has been carefully preserved and is the home of a thriving artistic community. There are many small art galleries, handicraft shops and restaurants. Visit the Museo Navarro Ramón in the Casa de Cultura, on Calle Ibáñez (see **MUSEUMS**). The sailing club is one of the best on the coast and has excellent sports facilities. Altea is also known locally for its high-quality, expensive fashion boutiques on the Avenida Fermín

Sanz Orrio, and its lively open-air market (see **A-Z**). Bus services:
hourly to Alicante and Benidorm. Train services: Connections to nearby
coastal towns by the narrow-gauge *Lemon Train* (see **Railways**). See
EXCURSION 1, RESORT REVIEW 1.

Babysitters: The best way to find a reliable babysitter is to ask at
your hotel. Two or three days' notice may be required during the high
season and you can expect to pay 500ptas per hr. See **Children**.

Banks: They are plentiful in the major towns and offer all the customary services. Their charges for exchanging currency are likely to be
lower than the *bureaux de change*. See **Money**.

Beaches: The best beaches on the Costa Blanca are north of Alicante,
with the undisputed champions being the large twin beaches of
Benidorm. South of Alicante, the coastline is generally less developed
and from Santa Pola (see **RESORT REVIEW 2, A-Z**) to Mar Menor (see
RESORT REVIEW 2, A-Z) the beaches are long and featureless, with fewer
facilities. The standard of cleanliness is good throughout, with several
beaches boasting the European clean beach insignia of the blue flag.
See **BEACHES**.

Benidorm: 42 km north east of Alicante. From a winter population of 35,000 people, Benidorm swells in the months of July, August and September to accommodate 450,000 holiday-makers, 40% of these Spanish and 23% British. By far the busiest, most cosmopolitan city on the Costa Blanca, Benidorm was developed in the early 1960s around its two magnificent beaches (see **BEACHES 2**). These are well worth a visit, particularly in May or early June, before the annual crush begins. The city's famous nightlife scene is a mixture of the highly sophisticated and the highly crass, ranging from the Casino Costa Blanca and the Benidorm Palace to the grotesque caricature English bars of the Calle de Gerona. To see Benidorm as it once was, visit the old town, now mostly spoiled by overdevelopment but still retaining many interesting and authentic Spanish bars and restaurants. Still in the old town area, look out to sea from the pretty Balcón de Mer, below the old church. To the west of the town, the attractive and busy Poniente beach is flanked by whitewashed residential villas and parks, and near the Balcón de Mer there is a small yachting harbour. Cruises are available from here to the Isla de Benidorm. Bus services: hourly to Alicante and regularly to the main towns and villages along the coast and inland. Train services: connections to coastal towns between Alicante and Denia (see **RESORT REVIEW 1**, **A-Z**) by the narrow-gauge *Lemon Train* (see **Railways**). See **RESORT REVIEW 1**, **BENIDORM**.

Bicycle Hire: You will find bicycles for hire in the main tourist resorts such as Benidorm, Moraira, Villajoyosa, Jávea, Denia, Santa Pola, Torrevieja and La Manga del Mar Menor.

Boat Services and Trips: There is a regular ferry service from Alicante to the Balearic Islands and also to Oran in Algeria. Contact: *Compañía Transmediterránea*, Explanada de España 2, tel: 20 60 11. A regular boat service operates between Denia (see **RESORT REVIEW 1**, **A-Z**) and Ibiza. Contact: *Compañía Isnada*, tel: 78 41 00 (from Denia), 30 40 96 (from Ibiza). Reservations are advisable during the high season. In addition, there are trips from Alicante to the Isla de Tabarca (see **MUSTS**, **A-Z**) in summer and from Santa Pola (see **RESORT REVIEW 2**, **A-Z**) to Tabarca all year round.

Budget:

Continental Breakfast	250-500ptas.
Full Breakfast	500-600ptas.
Lunch	500ptas (dish of the day in a restaurant).
Dinner	1500-3000ptas.
Wine (bottle)	235ptas (supermarket), 500ptas (restaurant).
Beer	70-100ptas.
Soft Drinks	125ptas per litre.
Discos	600-800ptas.
Museums	200ptas.

Bullfighting: The origins of this spectacle are obscure, but the rules for bullfighting as it is today were established during the 18thC. It is not a sport, but rather a stylized art form, deeply rooted in Spanish culture. The bloodshed involved as the bull is weakened by the insertion of lances and darts before being killed by the matador is not to everyone's liking, but many are fascinated by the colour and drama of the ritual encounter. Most large towns have a Plaza de Toros, a circular arena which can accommodate up to 25,000 people. The seats are classified as *sombra* (shaded), *sol y sombra* (shaded for the latter part of the *corrida*), and *sol* (sunny). Prices vary accordingly, *sombra* being the most expensive. In summer, temporary arenas are set up on village squares during the fiestas and visitors may watch either bullfights or informal *capeas* performed by lesser names and trainees. Tourists may also see bullfighting without blood in Benidorm (see **BENIDORM 2**). *Corridas* are advertized on street panels at least one or two weeks before the fight.

Buses: The Costa has the following daily return services: Alicante to Valencia 8 times; Alicante to Benidorm 8 times; Alicante to Denia 4 times; Alicante to Jávea (via Gata de Gorgos) twice; Alicante to Jávea (via Teulada) twice; Alicante to Torrevieja twice; Alicante to Guardamar del Segura once. Each resort has its own municipal network serving neighbouring beaches and tourist accommodation areas. Services cease operating at 2000. Coach tickets are more expensive than the narrow-gauge *Lemon Train* (see **Railways**) but much cheaper than the regular trains. In Alicante the Estación Central de Autobuses is located between the Calle Pintor Lorenzo Casanova and Calle Italia and for the longer journeys you will need to book your seat before you get onto the coach. In Benidorm the coach stop is on Avenida Jaime I (Carretera de Circunvalación).

Calpe: Pop. 8000. 65 km north east of Alicante, 20 km north east of Benidorm. A fishing village and tourist centre at the foot of the dramatic 327 m high crag, the Peñón de Ifach (see **WALK 4**, **A-Z**). Visit the old part of town on top of the hill, the small port on one side of the Peñón and, on the other side, the remains of Roman baths on the Paseo Marítimo. There are several good beaches in and around the town (see **BEACHES 2**). Bus services: Hourly to Alicante, Benidorm, Denia (see **RESORT REVIEW 1**, **A-Z**) and Valencia (see **WHAT TO SEE 3**, **A-Z**). Trains: The narrow-gauge *Lemon Train* (see **Railways**) carries tourists along the coast. See **EXCURSION 1**, **RESORT REVIEW 1**, **RESTAURANTS 1**.

Cameras and Photography: As you would expect in an area dependent on tourism, there are numerous outlets for buying film all along the Costa Blanca. It is generally of reasonable quality, and there are plenty of 24-hr developing services. Make allowances for the strong sunlight, especially when taking pictures near whitewashed walls or the sand and sea. Flash photography is prohibited in most churches and museums, and it is not permissible to photograph policemen, military installations or airport runways, for security reasons.

Camping and Caravanning: There are over 40 camp sites on the coast between Denia (see **RESORT REVIEW 1**, **A-Z**) and Torrevieja (see **RESORT REVIEW 2**, **A-Z**) and all the major resorts have at least two sites. These are graded from *lujo* (luxury) to 1, 2 or 3, depending on facilities such as swimming pools, children's playgrounds, shady areas, water sports and other sports, restaurants, bars, *etc.* Expect to pay about 250-350ptas per person per night in a standard two-person tent.
Local tourist information offices should be able to supply a list of camp sites in the area. See **Tourist Information**.

Car Hire: Local car rental companies are cheaper than the inter-national agencies. You must have a driving licence issued more than two years previously and be more than 22 years old. You will generally have to pay a deposit unless payment is by credit card. Third party insurance and tax are added to the rental. *Avis* and *Hertz* are at El Altet (see **Airport**) and *Ariel* are in Benidorm (tel: 85 03 43). See **Driving**.

Cartagena: Pop. 170,000. 115 km south west of Alicante, 157 km south west of Benidorm. The main Spanish military port on the Mediterranean coast, settled since the early 3rdC. It was formerly well protected by the (now ruined) fortress Castillo de la Concepción, built at the end of the 14thC on the hill dominating the city. Drive up and enjoy the panoramic view over the harbour, encountering en route the overgrown ruins of the 13thC Iglesia de Santa María. Cartagena is also worth a short trip to see the ships in the port and, on the seafront, one of the world's oldest surviving submarines, built in 1888 by a local inventor, Isaac Peral. See **RESORT REVIEW 2**.

Castles: There are several splendid castles on the Costa Blanca, but unfortunately, few of these are open to the public. The best are at Guadalest (see **EXCURSION 2**, **MUSTS**, **A-Z**), Santa Bárbara in Alicante (see **ALICANTE 2**) and Villena. Others of interest are at Denia (see **RESORT REVIEW 1**, **A-Z**), Santa Pola (see **RESORT REVIEW 2**, **A-Z**), Sax and Biar. The abundance of fortifications reflects the turbulent medieval history of the area, with castles frequently changing hands between Moors and Christians during six centuries of intermittent fighting. See **CASTLES 1 & 2**, **EXCURSION 3**.

Chemists: *Farmacias* are easily identified by their distinctive sign of a green cross. Opening hours (see **A-Z**) are the same as for other shops, with late opening determined by a rota system to ensure 24-hr service. Check in the window for the name and address of the nearest after-hours pharmacy. See **Health**.

Children: Children are well catered for in the larger resorts, with various amusement areas in public parks and on the beach. The Safari Parks (see **A-Z**) usually prove very popular with youngsters. See **Babysitters**.

Cigarettes and Tobacco: Local brands tend to be cheaper than international, especially the *Ducados* made from strong brown tobacco. Many international brands are made under licence in Spain and may not have the same flavour. Local cigars are cheap and of reasonable quality. Canarian cigars are better and excellent value. Cuban *puros* are available at reasonable prices. Cigarettes and cigars can be purchased from tobacconists (*tabacos* or *estancos*), news-stands, bars, hotels, and automatic machines in the tourist areas. Smoking is prohibited on all city buses and in cinemas, theatres, and administration offices.

Cinema: Most foreign films shown in Spain are dubbed. Showings in the original language with Spanish subtitles are advertised as 'v.o.'. Check the local listings to find out what's on, or enquire at your hotel.

Climate: The Costa Blanca has a Mediterranean climate - hot and dry in the summer, mild and with some rain in the winter. Most rain falls in spring and autumn with Murcia (see **A-Z**) being the driest area and Valencia (see **A-Z**) and Alicante the wettest, although rainfall is low, as is humidity. There are more than 3,000 hours of sunshine per year. Average temperature ranges: Jan.-Mar. 10°C-18°C; Apr.-June 15°C-22°C; July-Sept. 22°C-25°C; Oct.-Dec. 12°C-18°C.

Complaints: Hotels, inns *etc*, campsites, restaurants and petrol stations have to keep a supply of *hojas de reclamación* (complaints forms in triplicate). If your complaint is about price, you must first pay the bill before requesting the forms. One copy is retained by you, another is sent to the tourism department of the regional government. This is a valuable consumer protection measure which should not be abused by using it for petty complaints or grievances.

Consulates:

United Kingdom	Plaza Calvo Sotelo 1, Alicante. Tel: 521 60 22.
USA	c/ de Ribera 3, Valencia. Tel: 351 69 73.
Canada	c/ Núñez de Balboa 35, Madrid. Tel: 431 43 00.
Australia	Paseo de la Castellana 143, Madrid. Tel: 279 85 04.
New Zealand	consular services provided by British Consulate.

Conversion Charts:

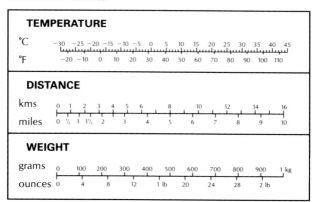

TEMPERATURE

°C   −30 −25 −20 −15 −10 −5   0   5   10   15   20   25   30   35   40   45

°F   −20 −10   0   10   20   30   40   50   60   70   80   90   100   110

DISTANCE

kms   0   1   2   3   4   5   6   8   10   12   14   16

miles   0   ½   1   1½   2   3   4   5   6   7   8   9   10

WEIGHT

grams   0   100   200   300   400   500   600   700   800   900   1 kg

ounces   0   4   8   12   1 lb   20   24   28   2 lb

Credit Cards: American Express, Visa, Eurocard and Mastercard, as well as traveller's cheques, are usually accepted in tourist hotels, restaurants, shops and travel agencies.

Crime and Theft: Certain simple precautions can be taken to prevent a theft spoiling your holiday: leave all valuables in the hotel safe; ensure that your hotel room, apartment or villa is securely locked when you leave; take care about flashing cash around and when leaving a bank; don't leave anything in sight in a car. If a crime has been committed, report it to the police immediately. Make sure to get a copy of your statement for insurance purposes. If your passport is stolen or lost, contact your consulate (see **Consulates**). See **Emergencies**, **Police**.

Currency: The unit of currency is the peseta (pta). *Coins:* 1, 5, 10, 25, 50, 100, 200, 500ptas. *Notes:* 100, 200, 500, 1000, 2000, 5000ptas . Old coins (with Franco's head) and the larger, ornate notes are no longer legal tender.

Customs:

Duty Paid Into:	Cigarettes	or	Cigars	or	Tobacco	Spirits	Wine
E.E.C.	300		75		400 g	1.5 l	5 l
U.K.	300		75		400 g	1.5 l	5 l

Dama de Elche: An enigmatic sculpture dating from c. 500 BC, the

Dama was discovered in La Alcudia, near Elche (see **A-Z**), in 1897. Despite the mystery of its origins and who or what it represents (it may not even be female), this unusual and impressive example of Iberian art is the province's greatest treasure. The original is kept in the Museo Arqueológico Nacional in Madrid, and replicas can be seen in the local archeological museum and the Huerta de la Cura (see **WHAT TO SEE 1**).

Denia: Pop. 22,000. 100 km north east of Alicante, 58 km north east of Benidorm. Denia takes its name from its Roman origins (Dianium). Denia is largely a modern town, popular with British tourists, and is surrounded by *urbanizaciones* (see **A-Z**) which are either self-contained or are close to one of Denia's many beaches (see **BEACHES 1**). Two old quarters have survived however: Les Roques, adjoining the castle walls; and Baix la Mar, the commercial and fishing district close to the port. See the Castillo de Denia (see **CASTLES 1**) and its Museo Arqueológico (see **MUSEUMS**). There are bus services to Valencia (see **WHAT TO SEE 3**, **A-Z**) and Alicante, trains to Benidorm and Alicante, and a boat service to Ibiza. See **EXCURSION 1**, **RESORT REVIEW 1**, **RESTAURANTS 2**.

Disabled: There is a new awareness of special needs, like toilets and ramps, but facilities are limited. Make full enquiries of travel agents or holiday operators before booking and clearly state your specific needs.

Drinks: The Spanish occasionally drink tea (*té*), with milk (*con leche*) or with lemon (*con limón*), but prefer coffee (*café*). *Café solo* is black, *café con leche* is half black, half hot milk. Mineral water (*agua mineral*) is either sparkling (*con gas*) or still (*sin gas*). *Horchata* is a sweet local iced drink, made from ground almonds, cinnamon and lemon peel. *Granizado* is iced, fresh fruit juice. Freshly pressed orange juice (*zumo de naranja*) is sometimes available but is often rather expensive. Spanish beer (*cerveza*) is very good and about as half as strong again as standard British lager. '*Una cerveza, por favor*', will get you either a draught 1/3 litre (about half a pint) or a bottle the same size and price. Wines and spirits from other parts of Spain include: *Cava*, good quality sparkling wine made by the Champagne method (*brut* is the best quality, other styles are very sweet); *Jerez*, the ubiquitous Sherry; *Coñac*, Spanish brandy, ranging from sweet and heavy, eg *Fundador*, to light and dry - try the *103* brand for one in between; *sangría*, a beach party cocktail of red wine, brandy and fruit topped up with ice and soda. French liqueurs are common. Many are made under licence in Spain and are consequently cheap. See also **Wine**.

Driving: When driving in Spain you will need your passport and current driving licence (international or EC). If bringing your own vehicle you will also need its registration certificate, a minimum of third party insurance, which a green card (available from the AA or RAC) will provide, and bail bond (usually issued with green card). You will need to carry a red warning triangle if going on a motorway. The primary road network is good and improving all the time. Be alert on secondary roads in the mountains because of the speed of the local drivers. Safety belts must be worn and children under 13 must sit on the back seat. Drive on the right and overtake on the left. Speed limits are: 120 kph on motorways (currently only the A7), 100 kph on main roads, 90 kph on other roads and 60 kph in built-up areas. See **Accidents and Breakdowns**, **Car Hire**, **Garages**, **Petrol**.

Drugs: Possession of drugs is illegal and anyone caught bringing drugs into the country will be subject to harsh penalties. The more liberal policies of the early 1980s have hardened to prevent drugs, and the associated crime, becoming a problem.

Elche: Pop. 164,000. 23 km south west of Alicante, 65 km south west of Benidorm. A bustling, modern city famous for the largest plantation of date palms in Europe, first planted 300 BC and watered by Abderraman III's 10thC irrigation system. The Huerta de la Cura (Priest's Grove) is the magnificent centrepiece collection of cactus, pomegranate and orange trees.

Overlooking the grove's lily-pond is an exact replica of the bust of the *Dama de Elche* (see **A-Z**). The centre of the city boasts splendid remains from the 14th, 15th and 16thCs clustered around the huge 17thC Baroque basilica, Iglesia de Santa María. Modern Elche is famous locally for its excellent value fashionable footwear and its large regional market (see **A-Z**). It also has many fashionable shopping streets around the main square, La Glorieta. The town is also synonymous with the *Misterio de Elche* (see **A-Z**), a sacred lyrical drama, dating from the 13thC, performed on 13-15 August in the basilica. Trains: to Alicante and Murcia (see **WALK 2**, **WHAT TO SEE 2**, **A-Z**). Bus services: hourly to Alicante. Public transport is recommended as Elche can be extremely busy for driving.

Electricity: Mainly 220V with round-pin, two-point plugs, so that adaptors are normally required for UK appliances. These are available in most large supermarkets at about 350-400ptas. In some older places the current is 125V, so be sure to check before you use an appliance.

Emergencies: *Police* - tel: 091; *Accident* - tel: (91) 441 22 22; *Policía Municipal* - tel: 28 47 65 (Alicante), 85 02 22 (Benidorm); *Fire* - tel: 22 90 81 (Alicante), 85 10 85 (Benidorm); *Hospital* - tel: 20 10 00; *Ambulance* - tel: 21 17 05; *Health emergency* - tel: 24 76 00; *Red Cross* - tel: 85 56 74 (Benidorm). See **Crime and Theft**, **Health**, **Police**.

Fauna: The Costa Blanca lies on bird migration routes so you may see a variety of birds at the appropriate times of the year. There are colonies of sea birds and peacocks on the Isla de Benidorm and flamingoes sometimes breed in the local saltpans too. The Albufera, a freshwater lagoon near Valencia (see **WHAT TO SEE 3**, **A-Z**) has plenty of duck and wildfowl, especially in autumn. The rivers hold a variety of fish, and sea fish include tuna and swordfish. In the hills there are deer, foxes, partridge, hares, *etc*. However, unless you actively seek out the local fauna, the only wildlife you are likely to encounter, apart from the animals in the safari parks (see **A-Z**), is the ubiquitous mosquito.

Fiestas: Fiestas are held throughout the Costa most of the year, but especially in the summer months. Typically, the streets and houses are decked with flags and bunting, stalls sell sweetmeats, the people enjoy themselves with music, dancing, processions and firework displays.
Alicante - 21-24 June: *Hogueras de San Juan* (see **A-Z**), parades, fireworks, bonfires and bullfights; 16 July: *Virgen del Carmen*; August: concerts in Plaza del Torre; 3-5 August: *Fiesta Mayor*, including the procession of the Virgen del Remedio, the city's patron saint, when the statue of the Virgin is taken out of San Nicolás de Bari (see **ALICANTE 2**) and paraded through the streets; 3-6 August: *Moros y Cristianos* (see **A-Z**).
Altea - 17-18 June: *San Antonio*; 21-24 June: *Hogueras de San Juan*; 15-17 July: *San Pedro y Virgen del Carmen*, procession of boats; 25-28 July: *Santa Ana*, procession, fireworks, concert, children's shows; 26-28 August: *San Luis*, *verbenas* (fairs), bonfires.
Benidorm - 21-24 June: *Hogueras de San Juan*; 29 June: *San Pedro*, popular acts and *verbena*; 1 July: *Fiestas de Verano*, musical and cultural festivals, including Spanish song festival and bullfights; 10 July: *San Cristóbal*, *verbena*, bonfires; 16 July: *Mare de Déu del Carmen*, boat parades; 25-7 July: *San Jaume*, song and dance festival.

Calpe - 21-24 June: *Hogueras de San Juan*; 16 July: *Virgen del Carmen*, boat parades, bulls in the port, bonfires, processions and dances.

Denia - 3 June: *Santísima Trinidad, verbenas,* dancing, bonfires; week incl. 24 June: *Hogueras de San Juan*; 29 June: *Baix la Mar* and *La Pedrera, verbenas,* dancing, bonfires; 6-14 July: *Boux del mar,* a 'bullfight' where the bull is not killed but briefly submerged in the sea, concerts, *verbenas*; 14-16 August: *Moros y Cristianos.*

Elche - 13-15 August: *Misterio de Elche* (see **A-Z**), mystery play.

Jávea - 21-24 June: *Hogueras de San Juan*; late July: *Moros y Cristianos*; 31 August-8 September: *Nuestra Señora de Loreto,* bulls in the port, parades, bonfires.

Santa Pola - 1-8 September: *Virgen del Carmen* (patron saint of sailors) and *Mare de Déu de Loreta* (patron Saint of the town).

Torrevieja - 11-16 August: *Fiesta de Habaneras,* musical competitions with competitors from all over Spain; 16 July: *Virgen del Carmen.*

Villajoyosa - 21-24 June: *Hogueras de San Juan*; 16 July: *Virgen del Carmen,* parades, *verbenas,* dancing, climbing a greasy pole; last week in July: *Moros y Cristianos.*

Fishing: Those of you interested in fishing may catch carp, bass and rainbow trout (though for the latter a special licence is required) in the rivers or lakes. Sea fish include mackerel, bream, bass, tuna, dorada and swordfish. Boats can be hired in Benidorm, Villajoyosa (see **RESORT REVIEW 1, A-Z**) and Altea (see **RESORT REVIEW 1, A-Z**).

Flamenco: One theory is that the original roots of *flamenco* to go back to the 6th-8thCs when it was a liturgic chant of the Visigoths. It evolved as the music and dance of persecuted minorities, such as Jews and Moors, and in particular gypsies, and was centred on the mountains of Andalucía. A full performance comprises *cante* (singing), *baile* (dancing), *toque* (guitar playing) and *jaleo* (rhythmic clapping and foot tapping). *Flamenco jondo* is profound and sad whereas *flamenco chico* is a joyous celebration of love. *Flamenco* floor shows (*tablaos*) take place in all the major resorts but aside from fiesta performances they are not heavily advertized so you may have to ask for details at the local tourist information office (see **Tourist Information**).

Food: Breakfast (*desayuno*) - Continental breakfast is the norm, comprising a selection of croissants, bread, jam and tea or coffee. Full English breakfast (*desayuno completo*) is widely available in the resorts. Lunch/dinner (*comida/cena*): The specialities of the Costa Blanca are fish, seafood and rice dishes (*pescados, mariscos, arroz*), combining notably in the national favourite, *paella*. This costs around 1600-1800ptas for two people. If you are on a budget or want to take the hassle out of ordering, most restaurants offer a choice of *platos combinados* (often shown by a photograph!), which is a good value, simple dish, *eg* pork chop or chicken with chips and vegetables or salad for around 500ptas.

Here are some local dishes worth trying:

Arroz a banda/caldera, rice cooked with seafood, then served on the side (*a banda*) with the same seafood. *Arroz negro* - as above blackened with with squid ink which adds a discreet scented flavour. *Emperador* - grilled swordfish. *Gazpacho* - chilled soup made from tomatoes and peppers. Various crudités are added when serving to make this an excellent starter. *Paella Valenciana* - rice cooked in stock, flavoured and coloured by saffron fried with either rabbit and/or chicken and pork plus vegetables such as peppers, peas, beans, *etc*. *Paella Alicantina* is similar, either substituting, or adding seafood to the meat content. *Zarzuela* - a rich stew of several types of fish and seafood in a tomato based sauce - this can be an amazing sight! *Pebereta talladeta* - tuna fish steak stewed together with potatoes and onions. *Guisado de pavo* - stewed turkey with potatoes, tomatoes, onions and fruits (particular speciality of Orihuela). *Oleta* - rice and various vegetables (praised by vegetarians). *Morro y orella* - rice cooked with pork muzzle and ears; rice is also served with rabbit, chicken and pigeon. Some seafood such as sea bass or congers is often cooked in a salt crust (expensive). *Calderos gazpachos* - the final 's' is important to distinguish it from the Andalusian *gazpacho* (chilled soup) - a spicy hotpot of chicken, pork, rabbit and (more rarely) snails, partridge or pigeon.

There are many special sausages made of pork blood mixed with onions, garlic and various herbs - *llonganizes, polltrota, sobresade* - usually served with rice or potatoes. Rabbit (*conejo*) is always excellent and usually cooked with tomatoes and onions. There are many roasted

meat delicacies but these are expensive - kid (*cabrito asado*) or young pig (*cochinillo asado*). *Cocas* are open pies containing sausages, vegetables or smoked fishes sold by the local bakeries (rarely available in restaurants) which make inexpensive and delicious snacks.
Turrón (see **BEST BUYS**) is made in Jijona (see **EXCURSION 4**) and is an Arabic delicacy made from minced almonds, orange tree honey, sugar and egg-whites. Other delicious sweets include *peladillas* (see **Alcoy**) and *pinyomets*, which are almond and pine seeds covered by a crust of sugar. See also **Tapas and Tascas**.

Gandía: Pop. 48,500. 70 km north of Benidorm, 112 km north of Alicante. The home of the infamous Borgia family. Visit the plaza with its medieval tower close to the Colegio founded in 1546. In the Calle Mayor you will see the Colegio church with its two splendid 14th and 16thC portals. In front of the church the facade of the Ayuntamiento (Town Hall) dates from 1781. The Palacio de los Duques was the birthplace and home of Saint Francis Borja (1510-72) who joined the Jesuit order. It is now a Jesuit college and there are guided tours of the impressive apartments with their exquisite tiled floors.

Garages: Spanish mechanics are very efficient and relatively cheap. Most of the major makes of car are well represented in Spain so obtaining spare parts is not usually a problem. Garages, as petrol stations, have to provide toilets, and keep them clean and in good order - you do not have to buy petrol to use the toilets. They are also legally obliged to provide a *hoja de reclamación* (see **Complaints**).

Golf: All the Costa Blanca courses are open to visitors and most of them will hire equipment for the day. It is best to phone in advance to book a round. All the following clubs are open all year round. Expect

to pay around 3500-4000ptas green fees per day (18 holes) plus 1000ptas if you hire a caddie.
Almaina Park Club on the road to Muchamiel, 34 km from Benidorm. 36 holes.
Tel: 521 23 06.

Campo de Golf Villamartín, Urbanización Villamartín, Orihuela on the road from Torrevieja to Cartagena. 18 holes. Prestigious club. Green fees 4000ptas per day. Hire charges - trolley 300ptas, motorized car 4000ptas, clubs1200ptas. Tel: 532 03 50.

Club de Golf Ifach, Urbanización San Jaime, Benisa, 13 km from Calpe on the road to Moraira. 9 holes.

Club de Golf Jávea on the road to Benitachell. 9 holes. Tel: 579 25 84.

La Manga Club, Los Belones. 36 holes. The two 18-hole Kentucky blue-grass courses are the best on the Costa Blanca. Tel: 968 569 111.

Penas Rojas Club, San Vincente de Raspeig, 15 km from Alicante. 18 holes. Tel: 524 12 66.

Guadalest: 70 km north east of Alicante, 28 km north west of Benidorm. Village inside a fortress built 547 m above sea-level. It was

constructed by the Moors 1200 years ago and is only accessible through a long tunnel carved through solid rock. The highest point is the cemetery which offers the visitor a spectacular view over the valley. The village is full of factories and souvenir shops carved in the rock. The best buys are shoulder wraps and shawls, lace, wool, pottery and wrought-iron art. Stop off at the famous El Mundo de Max (see **MUSEUMS**). See **EXCURSION 2**.

Hairdressers: A *peluquería* or *barbería* is where you go. The quality is good if you can overcome the communication barrier! Normal opening times : 0900-1300, 1630-2100. Closed Sunday. Appointments are necessary in the tourist centres during the summer.

Health: Make sure you have a travel insurance policy which provides accident and health cover. If you have to visit a medical practitioner or hospital you will be charged for their services unless you have a European Community health form E111 (available from the DSS), entitling you to free treatment.
All the main cities and tourist centres on the Costa have some English-

speaking hospital staff.
Alicante - Clínica Vista Hermosa, Avenida de Denia. Tel: 26 23 22.
Benidorm - Clínica Virgen de Fátima, Circunvalación. Tel: 85 38 50.
English, Dutch and French speaking staff. See **Emergencies.**

Hogueras de San Juan: Fiestas lasting three days and nights, 21-24 June, all along the Costa and particularly good in Alicante. There are exhibitions, processions, bullfights, fireworks, sports and fairs. On the 21st the bands play and sing all night, then the *planta* is erected in which the papier mâché effigies are displayed and where you can eat, drink and dance during the festivities. On the 22nd there is a colourful flower offering to the Virgen del Remedio. On the 23rd and 24th there are processions culminating at midnight on the 24th. The closing ceremony starts with fireworks and ends with the burning of the effigies.

Insurance: Before going on holiday, visitors are advised to take the usual precautions to protect themselves from expenses incurred by theft, accident or ill-health. See **Accidents and Breakdowns, Crime and Theft, Driving, Health.**

Isla de Tabarca: Pop. about 40 permanent residents. The island is 2 km long by 600 m wide. Ferries from Alicante (1 hr) and Santa Pola (30 min) service Tabarca. Formerly an ancient Moorish colony, it was occupied in the late 18thC by Genoese families expelled from their home island of Tabarka (off Tunisia). It has some interesting old 18thC remains and a quiet, wild landscape with many caves. The single sea-weed-strewn, pebbly beach, on the side of the island opposite the harbour, is its main attraction. Next to the beach is Spain's largest bank of solar power panels, recently installed as an EC experiment to power this isolated community without the need for mains electricity. There are no hotels on the island, therefore only day trips are possible. See **MUSTS.**

Játiva: Pop. 24,000. 100 km north of Alicante, 110 km north west of Benidorm. Also named Xàtiva (Valencian name). This was the birth-place of two notorious popes, Calixtus III and Alexander VI, who were

members of the Borja (or Borgia) family. The old part of the city is full
of fountains, huge plane trees, narrow alleys, escutcheoned mansions
and other examples of *Mudéjar* architecture. Visit the late Renaissance
Colegiata (Collegiate church) in the Calle de la Puerta de Santa Tecla,
with paintings by Jacomo Bao. Opposite stands the Gothic-style hospital with its ornate 16thC Plateresque portal. The old meat market El
Almudín, built in 1548, is now the Museo Municipal. Among its
exhibits are the 11thC Moorish fountain La Pila de los Moros and paintings by José de Ribera (born in Játiva). On the road to the fortress stop
at the 13thC Ermita de San Felíu which was built in pure Gothic style
on top of Visigoth ruins and contains a collection of primitive paintings.
The fortress dominates the hill above the city and is really two castles,
Castillo Mayor and Castillo Menor, dating from the 15thC.

Jávea: Pop. 10,900 (80,000 in summer), 92 km north east of Alicante,
50 km north east of Benidorm. Jávea is a sprawling town split into three
parts - the old town, the port and the holiday complex around Playa del
Arenal (see **BEACHES 1**). The old part is a maze of narrow streets and
whitewashed houses with arched porches, Gothic window frames and
wrought-iron balconies. Don't miss the Casa de Cultura (just off the
main square), a splendidly-restored, old galleried building housing a
library and café-restaurant. Visit the fortress Iglesia de San Bartolomé,
built in 1513 to protect the locals from pirates, and the Museo
Histórico y Etnográfico, set in a 16thC house off the square, open 1000-
1300, 1700-2000 Tues.-Fri. (mornings only at weekends and on holidays). Equipment for hire and lessons for all water sports are available
from the Club Náutico in the harbour. There is a good Tennis Club on
the road to Benidorm. Hire a small boat (or pedal boat) from Jávea or
Denia and see the interesting marine cave La Cueva Tallada. Bus services to Alicante, Benidorm and Denia (see **RESORT REVIEW 1**, **A-Z**). The
Lemon Train (see **Railways**) stops at Gata de Gorgos, 6 km outside
Jávea. See **EXCURSION 1**.

Laundries: Hotels usually take care of laundry. The prices are higher
than the local *lavandería* (laundry) or *tintorería* (dry-cleaner). Coin-operated laundrettes (*Launderamas*) are available in Alicante and Benidorm.

Market Days: At least once a week every town of any importance has a market offering local produce, handicrafts and sometimes antiques. Be prepared to haggle on non-food items and in the larger markets beware of pickpockets. *Monday* - Denia (tinned foods and gift items), Elche (Plaza de la Fruta, Plaza de Barcelona, Plaza de San José), Santa Pola; *Tuesday* - Alicante (fruit and vegetables), Altea (rugs, fruit, vegetables, flowers, crafts, clothing), Benidorm (fruit and vegetables), Callosa de Ensarriá, La Nucia, Orihuela; *Wednesday* - Benidorm (Avenida Filipinas, near Hotel Pueblo), Campello, Guardamar del Segura, Ondara, Petrel, Teulada; *Thursday* - Alicante, Jávea, Villajoyosa, *Friday* - Alfaz del Pi, Denia (fruit and vegetables), Moraira, Torrevieja, Finestrat, Gata, La Nucia, Orihuela; *Saturday* - Alicante, Benisa, Calpe, Santa Pola, Elche (Plaza de la Fruta, Plaza de Barcelona, Plaza de San José and Plaza del Raval, crafts); *Sunday* - Alicante (Plaza del Ayuntamiento, coins and stamps), Benidorm (Avenida Filipinas, near Hotel Pueblo), Elche, Plaza del Raval (crafts).

Mar Menor: 80 km south west of Alicante, 122 km south west of Benidorm. The Mar Menor is a large shallow lagoon covering 170 m², no more than 7 m deep at any point. These warm waters are almost cut off from the sea by a 22 km-long, 500 m-broad strip of sand known as La Manga, stretching from Cabo de Palos to the saltpans of San Pedro del Pinataz. Access to the sandy beaches (Marchamalo, Pedruco and Pudrimel) of La Manga is only from Cabo de Palos (see **BEACHES 4**). The main resorts are Santiago de la Ribera and Los Alcázares, where all water sports facilities are available. At the southern end there are yachting facilities - Los Nietos, Islas Menores, Mar Cristal and Dos Moros - with sailing and motorboat rental available for day trips to islands within and outside the lagoon. There is the excellent La Manga Golf Club (see **Golf**) and a horse-riding centre in Atamaria, 12 km south of Cabo de Palos on the road to Portman. Aside from sport there is little else of interest here. Nightlife is based around the hotels and includes the Casino Mar Menor where all the standard international gambling games are played. See **RESORTS 2**.

Misterio de Elche: The *Mystery of Elche* is a sacred lyrical drama dating from the 13thC, about the Assumption of the Holy Virgin. Sung in ancient Valencian by an amateur male choir, it is performed on the 14th and 15th August (dress rehearsal 13th) in Elche's beautiful 17thC Baroque Iglesia de Santa María. See **WHAT TO SEE 1**, **Elche**, **Fiestas**.

Money: The best exchange rates are given by the banks, although larger hotels, travel agencies and shops will accept traveller's cheques. Banks are open 0900-1400 Mon.-Fri., and some are also open 1000-1300 Sat. See **Banks**, **Credit Cards**, **Currency**, **Traveller's Cheques**.

Moros y Cristianos: To understand this colourful historical pageant requires a little knowledge of Spain's medieval history. In AD 711 Spain was invaded from North Africa by the Moors - a term subsequently given to all Arabs, Moslems and Berbers who came over to Spain. Within a decade they had conquered much of the country and so began a rule (tolerant and civilized) which was virtually unopposed for over three centuries. However by the 11thC the Spanish Christian forces had begun to re-establish their kingdoms and from then until the late 13thC saw the Reconquest and the decline of Moorish power. By 1492 the Moors had retreated to their last stronghold in the Alhambra and were finally driven out of Spain. The modern celebration is a homage to the local patron saint, with a symbolic and ritualized re-enactment of a large-scale confrontation between Moors and Christians connected in general terms with the Reconquest or specifically with a local battle. The basic programme always includes processions of militia in historical costumes ending in the recapture of a castle which symbolizes the town, and local participation in singing, dancing and general festivities. (*ie*, it is organized by the locals primarily for their own entertainment). See **Fiestas**.

Murcia: Pop. 290,000. 77 km south west of Alicante, 119 km south west of Benidorm. Capital of the province of the same name, Murcia is a large, modern, prosperous city. At its heart, however, the magnificent Catedral de Santa María still dominates the old quarter which is filled with attractive, ancient buildings. There are several good museums and good shopping in the Calle de la Trapería. A large annual fair is held from 1-15 September to celebrate the return to the city after the summer holidays. Major bullfights take place every night during the first week. Just outside Murcia at Monteagudo is a giant statue of Christ with outstretched arms, a copy of the famous work in Rio de Janeiro. See **WALK 2, WHAT TO SEE 2**.

Newspapers and Magazines: In the tourist areas most newsstands have the main European papers one day after publication.

English versions of Spanish newspapers are published in the summer and English, French and German weekly or bi-weekly local versions are also available. *The Costa Blanca Post* and *The Entertainer* are two free English weeklies.

Opening Times: In general:
Office Hours - 0900-1300,1600-1900 Mon.-Fri.; *Banks* - 0900-1400
Mon.-Fri., 0900-1300 Sat.; Museums - 1000-1300, 1700-2000; *Post
Office* - 0900-1300, 1600-1800 Mon.-Fri., 0900-1300 Sat.; *Restaurants*
lunch - 1200-1500, dinner - 2000-2400; *Shops* - 0900-1300, 1600-
1900 Mon.-Fri., 0900-1400 Sat., 0900-1400 Sun.

Orientation: The Costa Blanca ('White Coast'), extends from Setla (at
the south end of the Costa del Azahar) southwards, taking in the coastal
area of the province of Alicante. It consists of coastal plains with sandy
beaches and coves divided by dramatic cliffs. It is backed by small
mountain ranges which vary between 800 - 1500 m at the highest. This
book takes in the coast from Denia (see **RESORT REVIEW 1**, **A-Z**) in the
north to Puerto de Mazarrón in the south, including Benidorm and
Alicante. Valencia is also included (as an important city and place of
interest) although it nominally lies outside the Costa Blanca area.

Orihuela: Pop. 53,000. 55 km south west of Alicante, 97 km south
west of Benidorm. This old provincial bishopric hides a wealth of historic architecture in its narrow winding streets. Don't miss the Baroque
Colegio de Santo Domingo (church and college) which was built in the
16th-17thC. Its peaceful cloisters and staircase are open 0900-1300,
1600-1800 Mon.-Fri. The splendour of the 14thC Gothic cathedral is
second only to that of Murcia in the whole province, and (also like
Murcia) it contains a museum of sacred treasures including works by
Velázquez and Salzillo (1030-1230 Mon.-Sat.) Other buildings well
worth a look include the Iglesias Santas Justa y Rufina, the 18thC bishop's palace (1100-1300, 1600-1900 Mon.-Sat.) and the Biblioteca
Pública, Calle de Alfonso XIII 1, which is also the city museum and
contains the grotesque *Paso de la Diablesa* (she-devil statue), carved in
1688 by Nicolas de Busi (1230-1400, 1700-2100, closed Aug.).

Passports: Visitors holding a valid passport of an EC country or of
the USA and Canada do not require a visa to enter Spain. British
Visitors' Passports are also accepted. Visitors from non-EC countries
will need to obtain a visa as well as having a valid passport.

Peñón de Ifach: This immense rock reaches a height of 327 m above sea-level and is connected to the coast by an isthmus. It extends about 1 km into the bay of Calpe (see **RESORT REVIEW 1, A-Z**) and has a similar profile to the Rock of Gibraltar. A tunnel was drilled at a height of 180 m in 1918 and roads now drive to the top. From here on a clear day you can see Alicante (see **RESORT REVIEW 2, A-Z**), the Isla de Tabarca (see **MUSTS, A-Z**), Altea (see **RESORT REVIEW 1, A-Z**) Benidorm (see **MUSTS, RESORT REVIEW 1, A-Z**) and even Ibiza. See **WALK 4**.

Petrol: You will find four grades of petrol plus diesel on sale. The grades are: 85 octane, 90 octane (normal), 96 octane (super) and 98 octane (extra). 'Super' is the grade equivalent to four-star. Diesel is called 'gas-oil'. While there are many garages or petrol stations on the main routes and in the more developed areas of the Costa they can be few and far between elsewhere and it is advisable to top up when you can. See **Garages**.

Pets and Animals: It is not practical to take a pet out of Britain for a short stay as you will NOT be able to bring it back into the country unless it is left in quarantine for the prescribed period. If you are scratched or bitten by any animal during your visit, you should report the incident immediately and consult a physician. See **Health.**

Police: The *Policía Nacional* are the tough, smart-looking men and women in blue uniforms and berets who walk the streets in pairs and patrol in white or tan vehicles. Report any crime to them and make a formal statement at their *comisaría*. *Policía Municipal* (blue uniforms, white or blue cars) deal mainly with the city's traffic and enforcing municipal regulations. You'll see the *Guardia Civil* (green uniforms and tricorn hats) at immigration and customs posts and patrolling roads and rural areas. See **Emergencies.**

Post Office: If you want to use a *lista de correos* (*poste restante*) you will need to show your passport and pay a small tax to obtain your mail. Stamps may be bought from the post office, hotel reception desk, and tobacconists. There are no public telephones in post offices (see **Telephones and Telegrams**).

Public Holidays: 1 Jan. (New Year's Day); 6 Jan. (Epiphany); 19 Mar. (St Joseph's Day); Good Friday (moveable); 1 May (Labour Day); Corpus Christi (moveable); 25 July (St James' Day); 15 Aug. (Assumption); 12 Oct. (National Day); 1 Nov. (All Saints' Day); 8 Dec. (Immaculate Conception); 25 Dec. (Christmas Day). See **Fiestas.**

Railways: Spanish trains are usually comfortable and punctual, but not always clean. There are three types of trains: *Intercity* - used on national and international networks; *Expreso* - serving main stations only (1st & 2nd class); *Omnibus* - 2nd class only, with frequent stops. Alicante station, Paseo de la Explanada 1, tel: 22 68 40/45. A narrow gauge railway, Feve, known as the *Lemon Train* because of the groves it passes through, serves the northern Costa from Alicante (see **RESORT REVIEW 2, A-Z**) to Denia (see **RESORT REVIEW 1, A-Z**) and stops in all the main towns of the Marina Baixa (upper coast) and Marina Alta (lower coast). The station for Jávea (see **RESORT REVIEW 1, A-Z**) is at Gata de Gorgos, 8 km from the town itself. The Feve station in Alicante is at the start of the Avenida de Villajoyosa, tel: 26 27 31.

Religious services: Spain is mostly Roman Catholic but churches of many denominations are to be found in the tourist areas. The local press gives addresses and information on services.

Restaurants: The grading system for Spanish restaurants uses a 1-5 forks symbol to indicate the standard of luxury and comfort on offer, but note that it does not take into account the quality or value of the food served. In general the standards of hygiene and cleanliness across all restaurants and cafés is good. The only blemish is the local custom of throwing discarded *tapas* debris (see **A-Z**) - prawn shells, cocktail sticks, used serviettes - onto the floor after eating! See **RESTAURANTS, ALICANTE 1, BENIDORM 3**.

Safari Parks: The Costa Blanca has three safari parks, ideal for a day or half-day family excursion, all open every day of the year.
Río Safari Elche - 3 km from Santa Pola. A novel way of viewing the animals whereby small boats holding about 20 people meander gently along a water course through the compounds. Tigers, lions, elephants, camels, rhinos, hippos and monkeys are the main attractions. Some 6000 fully grown palm trees help to create the illusion of a tropical climate. The park is open 1030-2000.

Safari Aitana - 35 km from Benidorm. The largest wildlife park in Europe, Safari Aitana is set some 1000 m up in the mountains and covers 1.5 million m². Lions, tigers, elephants and antelopes all roam freely in a setting that is the nearest thing to the wilds of Africa.

Safari Park Vergel near Pego and Vergel off the N 332 Alicante-Valencia road. Over 600 animals roam freely here, including lions, tigers, zebras and elephants. There is also an aviary, a dolphin show and a well-equipped amusement park including aqua-scooters, go-karts and children's moto-cross. Open 1000-1900, 1000ptas, children 500ptas. Dolphin show at 1300, 1600, 1800.

Sailing: All the following resorts have a yachting club or sailing school (*Club de Regata, Club Náutico*) at the harbour, where boats can be hired: Denia, Jávea, Calpe, Altea (highly regarded), Benidorm, Villajoyosa, Alicante, Santa Pola, Torrevieja and La Manga del Mar Menor. See **RESORT REVIEW 1 & 2**.

Santa Pola: Pop. 12,000 (100,000 summer). 20 km south of Alicante, 62 km south west of Benidorm. A quiet town, not on the average British tourist's map, with several good beaches (which can get crowded) and good water sports facilities. Santa Pola is the largest fishing port on the Costa and is consequently famed for the quality of its seafood. Its 16thC castle is its most impressive feature and houses an archeological and maritime crafts museum plus an aquarium where small sharks and turtles mix in a colourful display. Open 1100-1300, 1700-2000 Tues.-Sun. Along the coast there are three watchtowers, built in 1552 by Charles I to raise the alarm if enemy ships were sighted - Torre di Pep, overlooking Santa Pola del Este; Torre de la Calerra, at the junction of the main Alicante-Cartagena road and the Santa Pola turn off; and Torre de les Salines, between the beaches of Lissa and Pinet. The *faro* (lighthouse) on the Cabo de Santa Pola gives sweeping views along the coast and across to the Isla de Tabarca (see **MUSTS**). There is a ferry to Isla de Tabarca every half-hour, 500ptas return trip.

Siesta: Between 1300 and 1700 most shops, businesses *etc* close for lunch and a sleep. Bear this in mind when planning excursions or sight-

seeing trips otherwise you will find everywhere shut. Smaller towns and villages in particular become ghost towns during the *siesta*. Restaurants and some souvenir shops will stay open throughout. Everything re-opens again by 1700 and closes between 2000 and 2100. The locals then stay up into the small hours.

Sports: Just about every imaginable sport is represented on the Costa Blanca, for either participator or spectator and at all levels of expertise.

The large resorts have an abundance of sports facilities where you can learn to play a new sport or brush up your existing skills. See **Fishing, Golf, Sailing, Tennis, Water sports**.

Tapas and Tascas: *Tascas* are bars which you go to as much for a drink, like a *caña* (draught beer), as something to eat. Many serve excellent *tapas* - appetizers, ranging from olives, nuts or crisps to small and tasty portions of meats, seafoods, omelettes, salads or vegetables. All are temptingly displayed on the counter so you can indicate what you want. Some are served hot. *Raciones* are larger portions.

Taxis: Taxis can be hailed in the street. Unoccupied taxis display a green light or a *libre* sign. Most taxis do not have meters so ask the fare before you climb in. Only four adult passengers are permitted per taxi. *Alicante* - tel: 10 16 11; *Benidorm* - tel: 85 30 42 or 85 30 38; *Denia* - tel: 78 34 98; *Jávea* - tel: 79 10 60.

Telephones and Telegrams: Telegram offices have erratic opening times and it is simpler to send telegrams by phone, tel: 22 22 20. In the tourist areas there are coin-operated telephone booths in the streets for local and long distance calls and also special (blue coloured) telephone offices run by a private telephone company, Telefónica, which are open until 2000.

Television and Radio: TVE1 and TVE2 have good-quality Spanish programmes and TVE3 transmits foreign programmes in summertime. Of the seven radio stations, Radio Ciudad Alicante (FM 93.2), Radio Benidorm (FM 102.9) and Radio Denia (FM 92.5) broadcast in English, French, German and Dutch during the summer months.

Tennis: Popular all over the Costa Blanca. Courts are freely available at most hotels whether you are a resident or not. As well as municipal courts, the larger towns have private clubs. In Benidorm, Altea and Villajoyosa alone there are around 175 courts! Expect to pay about 700ptas per hr for a court. The best equipped club is La Manga del Mar Menor with 15 courts (clay and grass). There are at least another 15 courts elsewhere in the Mar Menor area.

Time Differences: GMT+1 hr in winter; GMT+2 hr in summer.

Tipping: Restaurants include service charges in their bills but a tip of 5-10% is still customary, if the service and food has been satisfactory. Taxi drivers, tour guides and hairdressers also usually get around 10%. Other types of attendant expect between 25-100ptas.

Toilets: Although public toilets (*servicios*) are not that common outside the larger towns, nearly every bar and restaurant has a toilet for its customers. The standard of cleanliness is generally very high. It is considered impolite to use a bar's facilities without buying something.

Torrevieja: Pop. 12,300. 50 km south west of Alicante, 92 km south west of Benidorm. A well-developed, small seaside port popular with British tourists, its main attraction is its beaches (see **BEACHES 4**). There are good water-sports facilities at the Real Club Náutico and an aqua-park ideal for children just outside the town on the road to Orihuela, open 1000-1930 every day. Before 1500: adults 800ptas, 4-12 year olds 600ptas; after 1500: adults 600ptas, children 400ptas. Other sports facilities include horse riding at Club Hípico Torrevieja, Urbanización La Siesta, on the road to Crevillente. There is little else of interest apart from the old-fashioned casino on the front near the harbour, which boasts a grand painted salon and a *Mudéjar* entrance. Every Friday there is a traditional open-air market. Regular bus service to Alicante, Elche, Murcia and Cartagena.

Tourist Information: There is a local tourist information centre in every town along the Costa Blanca supplying information about accommodation, restaurants (although recommendations are not made), what to see and do, *etc*. They are usually signposted CIT (Centro Información Turística). Alicante also has an office that deals with the wider area of the Comunidad Valenciana, although the local office is more helpful. Although the staff are all friendly they are sometimes strangely reticent about giving you information so ask for everything they have got printed in English to get the most from them. Also beware of arriving in a new place where you need information during the *siesta* or at the weekend, as the offices will often be shut. *Alicante* - Plaza del Ayuntamiento, tel: 20 51 00 ext 212 (local information); Explanada de España 2, tel: 21 22 85 (Comunidad Valenciana information); *Benidorm* - Policía Municipal building, Playa de Levante, tel: 585 32 24; *Altea* - Paseo Francisco Franco, tel: 84 19 46; *Elche* - Parque Municipal, tel: 45 27 47; *Calpe* - Avenida Ejércitos Españoles 40, tel: 83 12 50; *Denia* - Patricio Ferrandéz, tel:78 09 57; *Jávea* - Plaza Almirante Basterreche, tel: 79 07 36; *Torrevieja* - Avenida Libertad II, tel: 71 07 22; *Villajoyosa* - Avenida del País Valenciano, tel: 89 30 43.
You can also get tourist information before your trip from the Spanish National Tourist Office at 57 St James's St., London SW1. Open 0915-1615 Mon.-Fri.

Traveller's Cheques: Many hotels will exchange traveller's cheques, but they offer less favourable terms than banks. You will require your passport for transactions concerning traveller's cheques.

Urbanización: A holiday complex comprising several apartments and villas. The larger ones are like enclosed communities with bars, restaurants and sports facilities. These are often open to the public.

Valencia: Pop. 745,000. Spain's third-largest city. Its history takes in the Greeks, Carthaginians, Romans, Visigoths and the Moors, from whom it was reconquered in 1283. It was the seat of the republican government from 1936-37. There is a large city centre with tiny, confusing streets. Among the attractions are the cathedral and the colourful flower market (Plaza del Caudillo). It is the capital town of the province and the old capital town of the kingdom. The busy port of El Grao is 4 km away. Tourist Information at Calle Paz 46. See **WHAT TO SEE 3**.

Villajoyosa: Pop. 21,000. 30 km north east of Alicante, 8 km south west of Benidorm. Ignore the heavy main road traffic and visit the old part of Villajoyosa by walking down beside the large church, through the arch marked Ayuntamiento de Villajoyosa (now the local police station). From here to the seafront are the multi-coloured houses which once served as landmarks for the fisherman, and with which Villajoyosa has become synonymous. Many of these are now weather-beaten and rather decrepit but if anything this adds to the old-fashioned maritime atmosphere of the town. The beaches, particularly those to the west, are Villajoyosa's main attraction and good water sports facilities are on offer at most of these (see **BEACHES 3**), particularly at the port, at the Club Náutico. If at all possible visit during the last week in July to enjoy the most spectacular *Moros y Cristianos* fiesta (see **A-Z**) on the Costa Blanca. The narrow-gauge railway runs to Denia (see **RESORT REVIEW 1**, **A-Z**) and Alicante (see **RESORT REVIEW 2**, **A-Z**). Hourly bus service to Alicante and Valencia (**WHAT TO SEE 3**, **A-Z**).

Water sports: Facilities for enjoying the water are plentiful on the north Costa between Denia (see **RESORT REVIEW 1**, **A-Z**) and Alicante, then scarce heading south until the Mar Menor (see **A-Z**) where they

become superabundant. Windsurfing is the most common pursuit and is available on most northern beaches, Water-skiing takes place at Altea, Benidorm, Calpe, Santa Pola, Torrevieja and the Mar Menor, but is expensive. Scuba-diving courses are on offer at Alicante, Altea, Benidorm (La Cala), Calpe, Santa Pola and Villajoyosa. See **BEACHES**.

Wine: *Vino* is *tinto* (red), *blanco* (white) or *rosado* (rosé). Spain produces some excellent wines in its Denominaciones de Origen, officially demarcated and controlled wine-producing regions, of which Rioja is the best known internationally, especially for its full-bodied, oaky reds. Many restaurants will have a *vino de la casa*, house wine. *Vinos de terreno* are simple, inexpensive wines from local bodegas, always best drunk young, which lubricate most fiestas. Before ordering a wine, see what local people are drinking or ask the waiter for advice. If wines are a special interest, invest in a good one. Wines from the Costa Blanca itself include *Utiel* and *Requena* (both red) from Valencia's hinterland and from the area north of Alicante: *Monóvar* (heavy red) and *Jumilla*, a strong (18% alcohol, most wine is around 12-13%) red wine. There is also the famous *Moscatel,* the sweet, white, dessert wine.